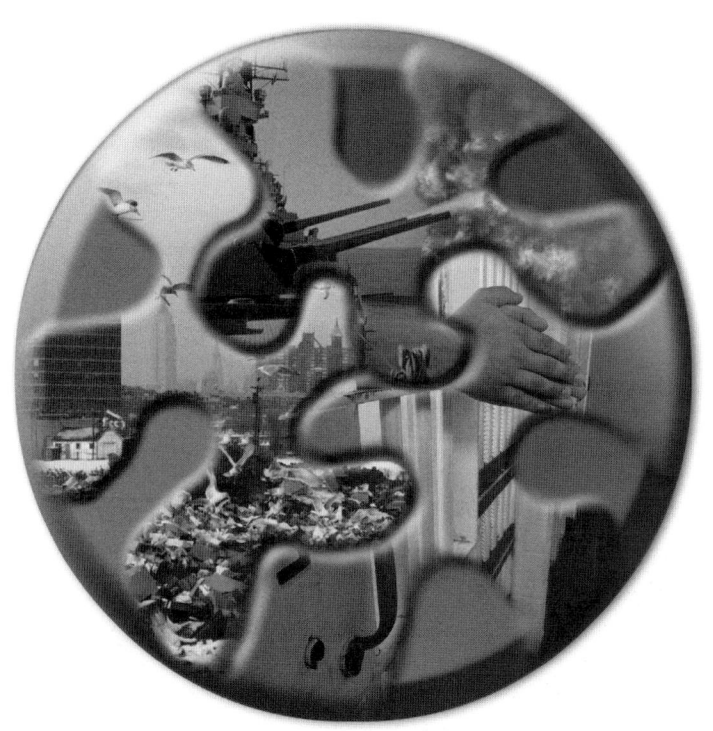

Religion and Society
Revision Guide

SECOND EDITION

VICTOR W. WATTON

Capital punishment + peace + conflict for Judiasm

Hodder Murray
A MEMBER OF THE HODDER HEADLINE GROUP

Hodder Headline's policy is to use papers that are natural, renewable and recyclable products and made from wood grown in sustainable forests. The logging and manufacturing processes are expected to conform to the environmental regulations of the country of origin.

Orders: please contact Bookpoint Ltd, 130 Milton Park, Abingdon, Oxon OX14 4SB.
Telephone: (44) 01235 827720. Fax: (44) 01235 400454. Lines are open 9.00–5.00, Monday to Saturday, with a 24-hour message answering service. Visit our website at www.hoddereducation.co.uk

© Victor W. Watton 2007
First published in 2007 by
Hodder Murray, an imprint of Hodder Education,
a member of the Hodder Headline Group, an Hachette Livre UK Company,
338 Euston Road
London NW1 3BH

Impression number 5 4 3
Year 2010 2009 2008 2007

All rights reserved. Apart from any use permitted under UK copyright law, no part of this publication may be reproduced or transmitted in any form or by any means, electronic or mechanical, including photocopying and recording, or held within any information storage and retrieval system, without permission in writing from the publisher or under licence from the Copyright Licensing Agency Limited. Further details of such licences (for reprographic reproduction) may be obtained from the Copyright Licensing Agency Limited, Saffron House, 6–10 Kirby Street, London EC1N 8TS

Cover photos courtesy of Corbis, Getty Images and Photodisc.
Illustrations by Adrian Barclay (Beehive Illustrations).
Typeset in 12/13.5pt Gill Sans Light by Dorchester Typesetting Group Ltd, Dorchester, Dorset
Printed and bound in Great Britain by Hobbs The Printers, Totton, Hants

A catalogue record for this title is available from the British Library

ISBN 978 0340 926833

CONTENTS

Introduction
How to use this guide — 1
Exam techniques — 1

Section 1 Religion and Social Responsibility — 4

1.1	The authority of the Bible	4
1.2	The authority of the Church	5
1.3	The role of conscience	6
1.4	Situation ethics	7
1.5	How Christians make moral decisions	8
1.6	The electoral system in the UK	9
1.7	Local government	10
1.8	National government	11
1.9	Different Christian attitudes to politics	12
1.10	The structure of the Welfare State	13
1.11	The Christian basis of the Welfare State	14
1.12	Non-religious arguments about the Welfare State	15

Section 2 Religion and the Environment — 17

2.1	The threat of pollution	17
2.2	The problem of scarce natural resources	18
2.3	Non-religious arguments about the environment	19
2.4	Christian teachings on creation and the environment	20
2.5	Christian teachings on stewardship and the environment	21
2.6	The teachings of a non-Christian religion on creation, stewardship and the environment	22
2.7	The work of a religious organisation in support of conservation	30
2.8	Animal rights	31
2.9	Non-religious arguments about animal rights	32
2.10	Christian teachings on animal rights	33
2.11	Teachings on animal rights in one non-Christian religion	34

Section 3 Religion: Peace and Conflict — 37

3.1	Two areas of conflict in the world today	37
3.2	Nuclear weapons and other weapons of mass destruction	38
3.3	Christian attitudes to pacifism	39
3.4	Christian attitudes to 'just war'	40
3.5	The attitudes to war of one non-Christian religion	41
3.6	The work of a religious organisation for world peace	44
3.7	The nature of bullying	45
3.8	Non-religious attitudes to bullying	46
3.9	Religious attitudes to bullying	46
3.10	Conflicts between family and friends	47
3.11	Christian teachings on forgiveness and reconciliation	48
3.12	Teachings on forgiveness and reconciliation in one non-Christian religion	49

Section 4 Religion: Crime and Punishment   53

4.1	The differences between sin and crime	53
4.2	The need for law and justice	54
4.3	Christian attitudes to justice	55
4.4	The attitudes to justice of one non-Christian religion	56
4.5	Theories of punishment	58
4.6	Christianity and punishment	59
4.7	One non-Christian religion and punishment	60
4.8	A religious prisoner of conscience	62
4.9	The nature of capital punishment	63
4.10	Christian attitudes to capital punishment	64
4.11	The attitudes of one non-Christian religion to capital punishment	65

Section 5.1 Religion and Medical Issues   68

5.1.1	Medical treatments for infertility	68
5.1.2	Christian attitudes to infertility treatments	69
5.1.3	The attitudes to infertility treatments of one non-Christian religion	70
5.1.4	Genetic engineering in humans	72
5.1.5	Christian attitudes to genetic engineering	73
5.1.6	The attitudes to genetic engineering of one non-Christian religion	74
5.1.7	Transplant surgery	77
5.1.8	Christian attitudes to transplant surgery	78
5.1.9	The attitudes to transplant surgery of one non-Christian religion	79

Section 5.2 Religion and Science   83

5.2.1	Biblical cosmology	83
5.2.2	Different Christian attitudes to the biblical cosmology	84
5.2.3	The cosmology of one non-Christian religion	85
5.2.4	The scientific cosmology	88
5.2.5	Christian attitudes to the scientific cosmology	88
5.2.6	The attitudes of one non-Christian religion to the scientific cosmology	89
5.2.7	Connections between science and religion	91
5.2.8	How some scientists see science as leading to, or supporting, belief in God	92

Full Mark Answers to Practice Questions   93

introduction

HOW TO USE THIS GUIDE

The aim of this guide is to help you revise and improve your exam skills so that you attain your highest possible performance in GCSE Religious Studies.

You should read the section on exam techniques first so that you know what types of questions are asked by Edexcel and what sorts of answers are expected. You should then work through Sections 1–4 which cover all the compulsory sections of the exam paper. If you are not doing coursework, you should then work through either Section 5.1 or Section 5.2 (whichever option you have been taught).

Sections 1–4 are sections of the specification on which you will have to answer questions in the exam. If you are not doing coursework you will also have to answer questions on one of the options in Section 5. Each section is divided into topics which you should use in the following way:
1 Learn the key words for the topic.
2 Learn the key facts for the topic.
3 Learn the main facts for the topic.
4 Do the practice questions at the end of the chapter and check your answers against the full mark answers at the end of the book to see how well you have done.

If your answers show that you are having problems:
- check whether your problem is that you cannot remember the facts. If it is, relearn the appropriate chapter.
- check whether your problem is that you have not answered the question properly. If it is, reread the exam techniques section below.

For Sections 2–5 you will only need to learn ONE religion other than Christianity. This revision guide covers Islam, Judaism, Hinduism and Sikhism, as well as Christianity.

EXAM TECHNIQUES

The examination paper is divided into five sections if you are not doing coursework, and four sections if you are doing coursework.

In each section you will have a choice of two questions:
- Section 1: question 1 or 2
- Section 2: question 3 or 4
- Section 3: question 5 or 6
- Section 4: question 7 or 8
- Section 5: question 9 or 10.

TECHNIQUES FOR CHOOSING QUESTIONS

Go through both questions in a section, ticking the parts of the question you think you can get a good mark on, giving more ticks for parts you feel more confident about. For example:
1 tick for (a), 3 ticks for (b), 4 ticks for (c), and 2 ticks for (d).

Add up the ticks you have given for each question and choose the question that has the most ticks.

Remember! You have to choose a complete question. This means that you must answer parts (a), (b), (c) and (d) from the same question.

TYPES OF QUESTIONS IN SECTIONS 1–4

All the questions have part (a) for 2 marks, part (b) for 6 marks, part (c) for 8 marks and part (d) for 4 marks.

PART (A) QUESTIONS

These are short-answer knowledge questions. You do not need to write full sentences for your answers. These questions often ask for the meaning of key words, for example 'What is stewardship?' so you will need to know the meanings of the key words for these questions.

PART (B) QUESTIONS

These are knowledge questions, which require a one or two paragraph answer.

They will usually begin with the words **outline** or **describe**:
- **Outline** means you answer broadly. This means you write one or two sentences about a number of issues. For example, 'Outline medical treatments for infertility' means write a sentence on each of the different treatments that are available.

- **Describe** means write in depth about one particular issue. For example, 'Describe what is meant by in-vitro fertilisation' means write a paragraph on this particular treatment.

If you are asked to outline different attitudes, it means you must write about at least two attitudes.

PART (C) QUESTIONS

These are all understanding questions and usually begin with the word **explain**.

You must go through the question and highlight the key words that tell you how to write your answer:

- **Why** means you must use the word 'because' and give reasons. For example, 'Explain why some Christians are pacifists' means you must answer in a way such as, 'Some Christians are pacifists because Jesus said in the Sermon on the Mount that Christians should love their enemies…' (then go on and give any more reasons you can think of).

When you see the word 'why' start singing the Wizard of Oz song so that you remember BECAUSE, BECAUSE, BECAUSE.

- **How** means you must connect two ideas. For example, 'Explain how the teachings of one religion other than Christianity could help people reduce pollution' means you must write out one teaching and explain how it could lead followers of the religion to reduce pollution, then write out another teaching and how it too could lead followers to reduce pollution and continue in this way.
- **Explain why there are different attitudes** means you must identify one attitude and explain why people believe it, then identify another attitude and explain why people believe that. For example, 'Explain why there are different attitudes to capital punishment in Christianity' means give reasons why some Christians think capital punishment is wrong, then give reasons why some Christians think capital punishment is right for some crimes.

PART (D) QUESTIONS

These are evaluation questions. They begin with a statement in quotation marks and then ask: 'Do you agree? Give reasons for your opinion, showing that you have considered another point of view.'

Even though the question asks 'Do you agree?', it is not enough just to give your opinion. You must:

- look at a view that is different from your opinion and say, with reasons, why people have this view
- state why you disagree with this view using evidence from your knowledge of Religious Studies
- come to a conclusion restating whether you agree with the question or not with a brief reason.

It is very important that you use religious evidence from the course and that you show you have thought about the statement before coming to a conclusion. Religious evidence could include:

- quotations from the holy book of one of the religions you have studied
- statements from religious leaders
- examples from worship or ceremonies
- statistics.

EXAMPLE OF A GOOD EVALUATION ANSWER

'All Christians should be involved in politics.'
Do you agree? Give reasons for your opinion, showing that you have considered another point of view.

a The view you disagree with, and your reasons
Some Christians would agree with this because they think Jesus showed this when he said in the Sermon on the Mount that you cannot serve two masters. Also St James said in his letter that Christians must show their faith in their actions.

b **Your view, with reasons**

However (this being a key word to show you are changing opinions; other words you could use are: 'nevertheless', 'on the other hand', 'others would say'), not all Christians agree with this. Some Christians believe that when Jesus said you should 'Give to Caesar what is Caesar's and to God what is God's', he meant that Christians should leave politics to other people and get on with serving God. People like monks are not involved in politics and yet they are surely Christians.

c **Conclusion**

So it seems to me that although it is important for Christians to help other people and love their neighbours, they can do this without being involved in politics, and so it is not true to say that all Christians should be involved in politics.

TYPES OF QUESTIONS IN SECTION 5

If you are not doing coursework, you will also have to answer one question from section 5. This section is marked out of 23, i.e. 3 marks more than the other questions. Each question is divided into three parts:

- part (a) for 4 marks
- part (b) for 8 marks
- part (c) for 8 marks.

You should spend at least 30 minutes on this question and it is a good idea to do it first so that you do not run out of time.

Part (a) is a knowledge question, the same as the part (b) questions in sections 1–4.

Part (b) is an understanding question, the same as the part (c) questions in sections 1–4.

Part (c) is an evaluation question, the same as the part (d) questions in sections 1–4, but marks are out of 8 rather than 4 and should have a longer answer.

The extra three marks are for your quality of written communication, so make sure you:

- write in sentences
- use paragraphs
- do not use bullet points or numbering
- take care with your spelling.

SECTION 1

Religion and Social Responsibility

1.1 The authority of the Bible

MAIN FACTS

Why the Bible has authority for Christians in making moral decisions

- All Christians agree that the Bible is the way to find out what God wants Christians to do.
- The Bible contains God's teachings on how to behave, such as the Ten Commandments.
- The Bible contains the teachings of Jesus on how to live, in such things as the Sermon on the Mount and the parables.
- The Bible contains the teachings of Christian leaders, such as St Peter and St Paul, on how to live.

Differences among Christians about the authority of the Bible in making moral decisions

- Some Christians would only use the Bible to make a moral decision because they believe that the Bible is the exact words of God dictated by God to the writers. Therefore it is the only authority for Christians.
- Some Christians believe that the Church has to tell Christians what the Bible means for today because they believe God still speaks to people through the Church.
- Other Christians believe that the Bible was written by humans and so is only a guide for making moral decisions. They think the Bible needs interpreting to fit what the world is like today.

KEY FACTS

Most Christians would use the Bible when making moral decisions because they believe that God speaks through the Bible and the Bible records what Jesus taught about behaviour. However, Christians have different attitudes to the Bible's authority. Some think it is the word of God and so is the final authority. Others think it needs interpreting by the Church and some think it needs interpreting to fit today's world.

KEY WORD

Bible the holy book of Christians with 66 books split into the Old Testament and the New Testament.

Remember
The first four topics of this section are about what help Christians use in order to make moral decisions.

1.2 The authority of the Church

MAIN FACTS

Although the Bible is the basis of all Christian moral decisions, most Christians believe that the Church needs to explain what the Bible means, and what Christians should do about moral issues.

How the Church decides on moral issues

1. Churches like the Church of England and the Methodist Church elect people to an Assembly which decides the Church's view about moral issues.
2. Churches like the Roman Catholic Church have leaders to make moral decisions. For example, the Pope and the Council of Bishops give teaching on moral issues to Catholic Christians.

Why the Church has authority

- Most Christians believe the Church is how Jesus Christ, the Son of God, works in the world, so it must have the same authority as Christ.
- Most Christians believe that God speaks to the world today through the Church.
- The Church is guided by God and so it must be able to make decisions on moral issues.
- If individual Christians made their own decisions on everything, no one would know which was the right thing for Christians to do. But if people follow the guidance of the Church, they can be sure they are doing the right thing.

KEY FACTS

The Church has authority because Church leaders are in the best position to say what the Bible means for today, and they always give guidance on moral issues. The Church is the final authority for Roman Catholics because the Pope and the bishops are believed to have special powers in interpreting the Bible.

KEY WORD

Church the community of Christians (with a small c, it means a Christian place of worship).

Religion and Social Responsibility 5

1.3 The role of conscience

MAIN FACTS

All humans have a conscience which makes them feel guilty if they do things which they regard as wrong, e.g. when you do something your parents disapprove of, you may feel guilty afterwards. These feelings of guilt are your conscience.

When should Christians follow their conscience?

The Catholic Church says that Christians should use their conscience as the final part of moral decision making. If a Christian's conscience says they should not follow the teaching of the Bible and the Church, they should follow their conscience.

Why Christians should follow their conscience

- Christians believe that the voice of conscience seems to be the same as the voice of God, therefore Christians should follow it.
- The Church says that Christians should follow their conscience.

Why some Christians think they should not always follow their conscience

- People have been mistaken about the voice of God, for example the Yorkshire Ripper claimed that God had told him to kill prostitutes.
- If Christians follow the teachings of the Bible and the Church, then they know they are doing the Christian thing.

KEY FACTS

Conscience is the inner feeling that makes people think something is right or wrong. Many Christians think conscience is the way God speaks to Christians today and so is the main guide for making moral decisions. Other Christians think it is safer to follow the Bible or the Church.

KEY WORD

Conscience an inner feeling of the rightness or wrongness of an action.

1.4 Situation ethics

MAIN FACTS

Many of those Christians who believe that conscience is more important than the Bible or the Church believe that Christians should follow **situation ethics**. This is a Christian idea from Joseph Fletcher. Accepting the authority of either the Bible or the Church means that things are either right or wrong whatever the situation. Fletcher felt that this was wrong and that Christians should base their moral decisions on Jesus' commandment to love your neighbour as yourself and on the situation.

Why some Christians would follow situation ethics

- Jesus seemed to follow situation ethics because he over-ruled what the Old Testament said when he thought it was unloving. For example, he healed people on the Sabbath.
- They think you should only do what will produce good results.
- They believe that Jesus' statement that the only laws are to love God and love your neighbour means that Christians should always do what will have the most loving results.

Why some Christians think situation ethics is wrong

- They think God would not have given laws in the Bible if they were not to be followed.
- They think the Church knows best what Christians should do.
- They claim you can never know all the facts about a situation. So what seems the most loving thing might not be if you knew more facts.

KEY FACTS

Situation ethics is the idea that the only moral rule Christians need is to love your neighbour. Christians who follow this believe that all they need to do when faced with a moral decision is work out what is the most loving thing to do in that situation. Other Christians think this can cause problems because you never know all the facts, or all the consequences of your actions.

KEY WORD

Situation ethics the idea that Christians should base moral decisions on what is the most loving thing to do in a situation.

1.5 How Christians make moral decisions

MAIN FACTS

To see how this is done, think of this situation:
A Christian has been invited to attend 'the wedding' of a friend who is 'marrying' their gay partner. The issue is, 'Should a Christian attend a homosexual wedding?'

1. A Christian who believes in the Bible as the only authority would not attend the wedding because the Bible says that men should not have sex with men.
2. A Christian who follows the authority of their Church in making moral decisions would make different decisions depending on what their Church teaches about homosexual relationships. An Evangelical Protestant Christian would not attend because their Church says homosexuality is a grave sin. A Catholic Christian might find it difficult to make a decision because the Catholic Church says it is not wrong to be homosexual, but it is wrong to have homosexual sex. A Methodist or a Quaker would probably attend the wedding because their Churches say homosexuals should be in a stable loving relationship similar to Christian marriage.
3. A Christian using situation ethics might say, 'The two men are clearly gay, they must also love each other to want to get married – to formalise their relationship and commit themselves to each other for life. Therefore the kind and loving thing to do would be to go to the wedding.'

KEY FACTS

When Christians have to decide what to do in a moral situation they can:
- use what the Bible says about it
- use what Church leaders say about it
- use what they feel is right (their conscience)
- work out what is the most loving thing to do (situation ethics).

Most Christians would use more than one of these.

Remember
Christians often use a combination of sources of authority to help them in making their decisions.

8 Religion and Social Responsibility

1.6 The electoral system in the UK

MAIN FACTS

There are two different electoral systems used in the United Kingdom.

1. First-past-the-post system

MPs and councillors are elected by this system. The candidate who gains the most votes is elected even though they may not have a majority of the votes cast. The arguments in favour of first-past-the-post are:

- It means that an MP or a councillor will represent a particular group of people and be able to deal with local interests.
- It usually produces a government from one party which many people think is more efficient than a coalition government (formed from several parties).

2. Proportional representation

MEPs and Assembly members are elected by this system. The seats are divided so each party gets the same percentage of seats as it got percentage of votes. The arguments in favour of proportional representation are:

- It means that a party has to have more than 50 per cent of the votes to form the government which means the wishes of the voters are represented.
- If no party gains 50 per cent of the vote, parties have to work together to form a coalition government leading to less extreme policies.

KEY FACTS

The United Kingdom has two ways of voting. MPs and local councillors are elected by first-past-the-post which some people think is best because people can vote for a particular person. MEPs and Regional Assembly members are elected by proportional representation which some people think is best because it makes sure that each party gets seats according to how many votes it received.

KEY WORDS

Electoral system the way in which voting is organised.

First-past-the-post the voting system where whoever gets the most votes wins the seat.

Proportional representation the voting system where seats are given as a percentage of the votes.

1.7 Local government

MAIN FACTS

Local government is funded by the council tax (based on the value of the property in which people live) and grants from the national government. It is responsible for:

- environmental services (refuse, street cleaning, etc.)
- leisure and cultural services (libraries, sports centres, swimming baths, museums etc.);
- trading standards (checking hygiene etc. in places selling food, checking that goods sold in the area meet national standards and rules)
- social services (children in care, care for elderly people, services for those with physical or mental disabilities)
- housing services (council houses, housing the homeless, organising housing benefits)
- planning and building (organising a development plan for the area; giving permission for all new buildings, checking all building work in the area)
- highways (maintaining the local roads, footpaths, street lighting etc.)
- registration of births, marriages and deaths in the area
- organising and checking street markets
- administering education, police and fire brigade (most of the funding comes from national government).

KEY FACTS

Local government is responsible for things that matter for the local area such as emptying dustbins, social services, leisure services, administering schools. There are different types of local government throughout the UK, including those responsible for a large area such as county councils and those responsible for just one village, such as parish councils.

KEY WORD

Local government the local council which looks after local issues such as education and refuse collection.

1.8 National government

MAIN FACTS

National government is the government of the whole country led by the Prime Minister and the Cabinet. Each member of the cabinet is responsible for a government department or ministry. The main departments are:
- The Home Office (the police, the prison service, immigration, asylum seekers, passports and visas).
- The Foreign and Commonwealth Office (UK's relations with other countries and the United Nations).
- The Department for Education and Skills (schools, colleges, universities, examinations and life-long learning).
- The Department of Health (doctors, hospitals, chemists, dentists and opticians).
- The Department of Work and Pensions (benefits payments, pensions etc.).
- Ministry of Defence (army, navy, air force and intelligence services).
- Department for the Environment, Food and Rural Affairs (DEFRA) (rivers and flooding, food production and standards, life in the countryside).

National government raises money through income tax, national insurance, VAT etc. Scotland, Wales and Northern Ireland have their own regional governments responsible for a variety of matters at regional level.

KEY FACTS

The national government of the United Kingdom is in charge of things for the whole country such as defence, the NHS, education, transport, law and order, pensions and benefits. It is led by the Prime Minister and Cabinet formed from the party with a majority of MPs.

KEY WORD

National government the government headed by the Prime Minister which governs the whole country.

Religion and Social Responsibility

1.9 Different Christian attitudes to politics

MAIN FACTS

Some Christians believe that Christianity and politics should be kept separate. They believe that Christianity is concerned with worshipping God, whereas politics is concerned with running the country. They believe this because:
- Jesus said some things belonged to God, and some to politics ('Give to Caesar what is Caesar's and to God what is God's')
- St Paul said that Christians should obey political leaders
- Church leaders like Martin Luther divided the spiritual from the material
- religion has to be kept out of politics in a multi-faith society because no one religion can be the most important.

Some Christians believe that Christianity cannot be kept out of politics and that Christians should bring Christian principles into politics. They believe this because:
- Jesus was involved in politics (e.g. when he threw the money-changers out of the Temple)
- Jesus taught that the whole of a Christian's life must be led by God
- St James showed that Christians must be involved in improving the material lives of other people
- Church leaders have all said that Christians should be involved in helping the poor, working for peace etc.

KEY FACTS

Christians have different attitudes to politics:
- Some Christians think that Christianity is about worshipping God, and politics is about running the country, so the two should be kept separate.
- Some Christians think that Christianity is about loving your neighbour and that means making sure that the country is run in a loving way. Therefore they think that Christians should be involved in politics.

1.10 The structure of the Welfare State

MAIN FACTS

The Beveridge Report (1942) into social conditions in Britain said there were 'five evil giants' facing society which had to be destroyed:
- **Want** – many people did not have enough to live on because they were unemployed, sick, widowed, etc.
- **Disease** – many people could not afford to see a doctor when they were ill
- **Ignorance** – most children left school without any secondary education
- **Squalor** – many people were living in slums
- **Idleness** – over ten per cent of the workforce was unemployed.

The Labour Government of 1945–51 established a Welfare State to attack these 'five giants' so that all United Kingdom citizens are assured of a basic standard of living and help from birth to death.

The main provisions of the Welfare State

The Welfare State uses National Insurance and taxes to provide such things as:
- free primary and secondary education for everyone, help with university education
- child benefits and family credits for families with children
- a National Health Service providing free doctors, hospitals and ambulances for everyone
- sickness benefit for people too ill to work
- weekly pensions for retired people
- payments and help with finding work for the unemployed
- means tested credits and benefits so that everyone has a minimum income and housing.

KEY FACTS

The Welfare State was developed during the 1940s to remove the evil giants of want, disease, ignorance, squalor and idleness. It is a system that helps everyone to have a good quality of life by providing such things as free education, free doctors and hospitals, payments for the old, the unemployed and the sick, help with housing, help with finding work.

Remember
The Welfare State is the system that helps everyone to have a good quality of life by providing things like schools, the Health Service and Social Security.

1.11 The Christian basis of the Welfare State

MAIN FACTS

The Christian Church has always felt it has a duty to educate children, help the sick and look after orphans and the homeless. Most of the reformers and politicians who worked to establish the Welfare State based their work on Christian teachings such as:

1. The Decalogue

The Ten Commandments in Exodus 20 say:
'Worship one God only. Do not worship idols. Do not swear using God's name. Keep the Sabbath day holy. Honour your parents. Do not murder. Do not steal. Do not commit adultery. Do not give false evidence. Do not covet other people's belongings.'

These commandments make Christians think about the needs of others. Honouring parents is like looking after the old. The National Health Service is a way of not killing the sick. Helping the poor and unemployed is not stealing from them. So Christians should support the Welfare State to keep the commandments.

2. The Golden Rule

Jesus said that the Golden Rule of the Christian life is to treat other people as you would want them to treat you. The Welfare State treats everyone in the way the rich like to be treated.

3. The Parable of the Sheep and the Goats

Jesus said that Christians should feed the hungry, clothe the naked and help the sick in the Parable of the Sheep and the Goats and this is best done by the Welfare State.

KEY FACTS

Most Christians support the Welfare State because:
- The Ten Commandments encourage Christians to care for the needs of others.
- The Golden Rule says Christians should treat other people in the way they would like to be treated.
- The Parable of the Sheep and the Goats says that Christians should help the homeless, the sick and the hungry.

KEY WORDS

Decalogue the Ten Commandments.

Golden Rule the teaching of Jesus that people should treat others as they would like to be treated.

1.12 Non-religious arguments about the Welfare State

MAIN FACTS

There are political arguments about whether the Welfare State should be for all (as in the British model), or only for the very poorest (as in the United States model where people are expected to have private insurance).

Arguments for the Welfare State
- It makes society fairer and gives the poorest people a feeling that they are part of society.
- It is an essential part of democracy for all voters to have the same rights to education, health care and a basic standard of living.
- It is more efficient. The National Health Service costs much less than the service that is provided in the USA by private insurance.
- Societies with a welfare state seem to make more progress than those without one.

Arguments against the Welfare State
- It takes the money from hard-working people and gives it to the poor.
- It forces people to contribute to the Welfare State rather than allowing them to choose.
- It takes away people's responsibility. For example, if people know the state will provide for them in their old age, they won't bother to save.
- Some economists think that economic growth does more for poor people than a welfare state. They claim that this requires low taxation and people being able to choose what to do with their money.

KEY FACTS

There are political arguments about the Welfare State. Some politicians think the Welfare State must be kept and improved because they feel it makes everyone feel part of society (which is essential in a democracy) and it is the most efficient way of creating a civilised society. Some politicians think that a lot of the Welfare State would be better provided by people sorting out their own health care, pensions, schools etc. because this will make people more responsible and lower taxes, thereby making life more efficient.

PRACTICE QUESTIONS ✓

a State ONE of the Ten Commandments. *(2 marks)*
b Give an outline of the Christian attitude that religion and politics should be kept separate. *(6 marks)*
c Explain why the Bible is important to Christians in making moral decisions. *(8 marks)*
d 'Your conscience is the best guide for deciding what is right and what is wrong.'
  Do you agree? Give reasons for your opinion, showing you have considered another point of view. In your answer, you should refer to Christianity. *(4 marks)*

Religion and the Environment

SECTION 2

2.1 The threat of pollution

MAIN FACTS

The Earth is an ecosystem where everything depends on everything else. Pollution can cause changes to an ecosystem which, in turn, can cause major problems.

The main problems caused by pollution are:

The greenhouse effect (global warming)
Burning fuels like gas, oil and coal makes carbon dioxide. This produces a barrier in the atmosphere which acts like the glass of a greenhouse – letting the sun's heat in, but stopping it from getting out.

This is making the Earth heat up (global warming). Some scientists think the average temperature in England will rise by 2 degrees Celsius by 2050. They think this will melt the ice at the north and south poles and cause massive flooding.

Acid rain
As well as producing carbon dioxide, burning oil, gas and coal puts more acid into the atmosphere so that the rainfall becomes acidic and can burn things. For example, forests in Sweden are being destroyed by Britain's use of fuel.

Eutrophication
The use of fertilisers on farms and sewage pollution are resulting in too much nitrogen entering streams and rivers making plants grow so fast that fish cannot get enough oxygen. The nitrogen also pollutes water supplies.

Deforestation
Trees are being cut down and not replaced. This leads to soil disappearing so that land becomes like a desert (desertification). It also leads to an increase of nitrogen and a decrease of oxygen in the atmosphere.

Radioactive pollution
Nuclear power stations have been built because they do not produce carbon dioxide or acid rain. However, they do produce nuclear waste which is buried in containers. This waste will take hundreds of thousands of years to become safe for humans.

KEY WORDS

Pollution the contamination/degradation of the environment.

Greenhouse effect the trapping of carbon dioxide in the atmosphere, which is thought to increase the Earth's temperature.

Acid rain pollutants, such as coal smoke, which make rain more acidic.

KEY FACTS

Pollution is caused by: burning oil, coal, gas; using fertilisers; cutting down trees. It is dangerous because it causes problems such as acid rain and the greenhouse effect, which could destroy the planet.

2.2 The problem of scarce natural resources

Oil is non-renewable because when it's gone, it's gone. Wind is renewable because it can be used over and over.

MAIN FACTS

Natural resources can be divided into two types:
Renewable resources are resources which can replace themselves after they have been used. They will not die out and using them causes no problems. Examples of renewable resources are: wind power, solar power, water power.
Finite or non-renewable resources are resources which are gone forever once they are used. Such things as oil, gas, coal, iron and tin are finite resources.

Finite resources are used for not only cars and heating, but also for everything made of metal or plastic. If we keep using these resources, they will disappear and there will be nothing to make cars, televisions, washing machines etc.

KEY FACTS

Resources are a problem because those which cannot be grown again (non-renewable resources), such as oil, natural gas and metals, will disappear. This will lead to major problems in our lifestyles.

KEY WORDS

Natural resources naturally occurring materials, such as oil and fertile land, which can be used by humans.

Environment the surroundings in which plants and animals live and on which they depend to continue living.

Conservation protecting and preserving natural resources and the environment.

2.3 Non-religious arguments about the environment

MAIN FACTS

There are many arguments about what to do about environmental problems.

1. Government action
Many people think the problem is so big that only action by world governments can help. In 1997, 55 industrial nations, including the United Kingdom, agreed to cut their greenhouse gas emissions by an average of 5.2 per cent a year (Kyoto Protocol). Many more countries have since joined including all the member states of the EU. However, the USA, India and China refused to sign.

The United Nations, and many scientists, feel that without international government action, global warming will end in disaster.

2. Science and technology
Many scientists believe that science and technology will find a solution to the problems:
- There are different ways of making electricity which do not produce carbon dioxide or nuclear waste (such as wind power, sea power, hydro-electric power and solar power).
- Car makers are looking at water, sugar cane and electric batteries as ways of powering cars. Using recycling can also help finite resources to last longer. Some cars are now made of almost 75 per cent recycled materials.
- Efficiency in some products has improved. For example, it took 50 small cars made in 2005 to produce the same amount of pollution that 1 small car made in 1976.
- Scientists are working on using chemicals from plants rather than oil to produce such things as plastics.

3. Alternative lifestyles
Some people think a change of lifestyle is the only solution. They think everyone should ride bikes instead of owning a car and stop using plastics, fertilisers, pesticides etc.

KEY FACTS

There are major arguments about environmental problems.
- Some people think that government action on recycling and reducing pollution and scientific action to find new fuels etc. will solve the problems.
- Some people think that the only solution is to change our lifestyles to stop the use of non-renewable resources and pollution causing activities.

2.4 Christian teachings on creation and the environment

MAIN FACTS

Christianity teaches that God created the universe and everything in it in such a way that it is perfectly suited for human life.

Some Christians believe the Genesis accounts of creation in six days are scientific fact. However, many Christians see them as showing that the Earth and everything in it was made by God in the way he intended it to be. As Genesis says, 'God saw what he had made and it was very good.'

Christianity teaches that, because God made the Earth, the Earth belongs to God.

How Christian beliefs about creation affect attitudes to the environment

- The environment must be respected by humans because it has been made by God and is a gift from God.
- God created the environment as something which is good, therefore Christians have a duty to preserve the environment.

KEY FACTS

Christians believe that the world, and everything in it, was created by God and so is good and sacred. Therefore it must be respected and cared for by humans.

KEY WORD

Creation the act of creating the universe, or the universe which has been created.

2.5 Christian teachings on stewardship and the environment

MAIN FACTS

In the Genesis accounts of creation, God gave humans the right to rule over the Earth. Therefore they are stewards of the Earth. The Old Testament also teaches that humans have a responsibility to treat animals well.

Many Christians think the teaching of Jesus in the Parable of the Talents or Minas (*Luke 19:11–26*) means Christians have a responsibility to leave the Earth a better place than they found it.

Jesus taught that Christians have a responsibility to make sure the Earth's resources are shared fairly. Most Christians believe that they will be judged by God on how well they have fulfilled their duty as stewards of God's Earth.

How Christian beliefs about stewardship affect attitudes to the environment

- The responsibility to be God's stewards and to leave the Earth a better place than they found it means that Christians should try to reduce pollution and preserve resources.
- Christians should show stewardship by working to share the Earth's resources more fairly and improve the standard of living in LEDCs (Less Economically Developed Countries).
- The belief that they will be judged on their behaviour as stewards means Christians should help the work of groups which try to reduce pollution and conserve resources.

However, Christians believe human interests come first, for example shutting down a factory which causes pollution but employs three thousand people would not be a Christian solution.

KEY FACTS

Christians believe that God made humans to look after the world as his stewards – to have authority over animals and plants. However, the Bible teaches that Christians should care for the environment and leave the Earth a better place than they found it.

KEY WORD

Stewardship looking after something so that it can be passed on to the next generation.

2.6 The teachings of a non-Christian religion on creation, stewardship and the environment

Islam and creation

MAIN FACTS

Islam teaches that the universe and everything in it was created by God as a place perfectly suited for human life.

One of the most important Muslim beliefs is called Tawhid. This means that there is only one God and so there is a unity in creation. This unity can be seen in the way in which the universe runs on scientific laws.

The Qur'an teaches that there is a balance in the universe which is like the whole universe being a huge ecosystem.

How Islamic teachings about creation affect attitudes to the environment

- The whole environment must be respected because it has been made by God as a gift to humans.
- God made a unity and balance in creation, so Muslims have a duty to preserve the environment and keep the balance.

KEY FACTS

Muslims believe that the world, and everything in it, was created by God and so is good and sacred. So it must be respected and cared for by humans.

2.6 The teachings of a non-Christian religion on creation, stewardship and the environment

Islam and stewardship

MAIN FACTS

Islam teaches that God created Adam as his khalifah to look after the Earth for God. This means that all Muslims are God's khalifahs who have to keep the balance of creation and look after the Earth for God in the way set out in the Qur'an and the Shari'ah.

Islam also teaches that people will be judged by God on the way they have looked after the Earth and the life on Earth.

This life is a test from God. A main part of the test is looking after the environment in the way of Islam. Those who fail the test will be punished.

How Islamic teachings about stewardship affect attitudes to the environment

- The responsibility to be God's khalifah means that Muslims should try to reduce pollution and preserve resources.
- The ummah means Muslim stewardship includes a fair sharing of the Earth's resources, so Muslims should work to share the Earth's resources more fairly and improve the standard of living in LEDCs.
- The belief that they will be judged on their behaviour as khalifahs means Muslims have a duty to help the work of groups which try to reduce pollution and conserve resources.

However, Muslims believe that human interests come first and so the effects of environmental projects on humans cannot be ignored.

KEY FACTS

Islam teaches that God created humans as his stewards of the Earth. He showed people how to look after the Earth in the Qur'an. Life is a test and God will judge Muslims on how well they have looked after the world.

Remember
Khalifah means steward – someone who looks after things for you.

2.6 The teachings of a non-Christian religion on creation, stewardship and the environment

Judaism and creation

MAIN FACTS

Judaism teaches that God created the universe and everything in it in such a way that it is perfectly suited for human life.

Some Jews believe the Genesis accounts of creation in six days are scientific fact. However, many Jews see them as showing that the Earth and everything in it was made by God in the way he intended it to be. As Genesis says, 'God saw what he had made and it was very good.'

Judaism teaches that, because God made the Earth, the Earth belongs to God.

How Jewish beliefs about creation affect attitudes to the environment

- The environment must be respected by humans because it has been made by God and is a gift from God.
- God created the environment as something which is good, therefore Jews have a duty to preserve the environment.

KEY FACTS

Jews believe that the world, and everything in it, was created by God and so is good and sacred. So it must be respected and cared for by humans.

2.6 The teachings of a non-Christian religion on creation, stewardship and the environment

Judaism and stewardship

MAIN FACTS

Judaism teaches that God made humans as stewards of his Earth and gave them control of the Earth and all its creatures. However, as God's stewards, Jews must look after the Earth in the way God intended:

- Numbers 35:2 says that around every town there must be an area of open parkland.
- Respect for the land and for trees is shown in the special Jewish festival of New Year for Trees when trees are planted in areas where they are needed.
- Leviticus 25 orders Jews that every 50 years they must not plant crops or harvest such things as fruit trees – nature must have a chance to recharge its batteries.
- All these teachings are based on mitzvot in the Torah and Jews believe they will be judged by God on how well they have followed the mitzvot.

How Jewish teachings about stewardship affect attitudes to the environment

- The responsibility to be God's stewards and to leave the Earth a better place than they found it means that Jews should try to reduce pollution and preserve resources.
- Jews should show stewardship by working to share the Earth's resources more fairly and improve the standard of living in LEDCs.
- The belief that they will be judged on their behaviour as stewards means Jews should help the work of groups which try to reduce pollution and conserve resources.

However, Jews believe that human interests come first and so the effects of environmental projects on humans cannot be ignored.

KEY FACTS

Judaism teaches that God created humans as his stewards of the Earth to have authority over animals and plants. He showed people how to look after the Earth in the mitzvot. Life is a test and God will judge Jews on how well they have looked after the world.

Remember
Mitzvot are God's laws for the Jewish people.

2.6 The teachings of a non-Christian religion on creation, stewardship and the environment

Hinduism and creation

> **MAIN FACTS**
>
> There are two Hindu attitudes to creation:
> - some Hindus believe that God created the universe
> - other Hindus believe that the universe is a part of God and has always existed.
>
> Whatever attitude they have, Hindus believe that God is present in nature and so is a part of the Earth. This means humans should try to find God in nature.
>
> #### How Hindu teachings about creation affect attitudes to the environment
> - As everything is a part of God, the whole environment must be respected by humans.
> - The need for humans to find God in nature means that Hindus have a duty to preserve the environment and make sure that it continues to be what God intended it to be.
>
> **KEY FACTS**
>
> Hindus believe that the world, and everything in it, is a part of God and so is good and sacred. So the whole environment must be respected and cared for by humans.

2.6 The teachings of a non-Christian religion on creation, stewardship and the environment

Hinduism and stewardship

MAIN FACTS

Many Hindus would not talk about being stewards of the Earth, but all Hindus have certain duties towards the Earth. Hindu beliefs about looking after the Earth include:
- **Respect for animal life.** The fact that many Hindu gods have appeared as animals, and that people may have been animals in previous lives, means animals must be respected and many Hindus are vegetarian.
- **Respect for nature.** Trees and nature are very special because the last stage of life is to live in the forest to find union with God.

How Hindu teachings about stewardship affect attitudes to the environment
- The need to find God in nature means that Hindus should try to reduce pollution.
- The appearances of the gods as animals mean protecting animals and being vegetarian.
- Hindus should show stewardship by working to share the Earth's resources more fairly and improve the standard of living in LEDCs.
- The belief in respect for life means Hindus should help the work of groups which try to reduce pollution and conserve resources.

Although Hindus should have a great respect for the environment, some Hindus feel that humans have the right to use the Earth's resources in any way they think is right. There is a lot of argument in India about industry and the environment.

KEY FACTS

Hindus believe they have a duty to show stewardship towards the Earth. The avatars of the gods as animals mean that Hindus should respect and look after animals. The law of nature and respect for life mean that Hindus should reduce pollution and try for a fair sharing of resources. However, some Hindus believe the interests of humans should come first.

Remember
Hindus talk about respect for the Earth rather than stewardship of the Earth.

2.6 The teachings of a non-Christian religion on creation, stewardship and the environment

Sikhism and creation

MAIN FACTS

Sikhism teaches that, before He created the Universe, God existed all alone. Then God willed the creation of the universe to please Himself, and to spread himself throughout the universe.

This teaching means that God is present in nature and so is a part of the Earth. There is a oneness in the universe and in nature.

How Sikh teachings about creation affect attitudes to the environment

- As God is spread throughout nature, the whole environment must be respected by humans.
- The universe contains God and so nature can be a means to find God. This means that Sikhs have a duty to preserve the environment.

KEY FACTS

Sikhs believe that the world, and everything in it, is a part of God and so is good and sacred. So the whole environment must be respected and cared for by humans.

2.6 The teachings of a non-Christian religion on creation, stewardship and the environment

Sikhism and stewardship

MAIN FACTS

Although Sikhs do not always talk about being stewards of the Earth, they do feel that they have a duty to look after the Earth. There are many stories of the Gurus acting as stewards of the Earth: Sikhs should follow the examples of the Gurus, and act as stewards of the Earth.

Sikh beliefs about stewardship include: respect for nature, keeping sound ecosystems, reducing pollution, respect for animal life.

How Sikh teachings about stewardship affect attitudes to the environment

- The examples of the Gurus make most Sikhs believe that they should protect animals and create and preserve ecosystems.
- Sikhs should show stewardship by working to share the Earth's resources more fairly and improve the standard of living in LEDCs.
- The belief in respect for life means Sikhs should help the work of groups which try to reduce pollution and conserve resources.

Although Sikhs should have a great respect for the environment, some Sikhs feel that in arguments between environmental protection and human jobs and living standards, the rights of humans should come first.

KEY FACTS

Sikhs believe they have a duty to show stewardship towards the Earth. The examples of the Gurus mean that Sikhs should respect and look after animals. Respect for God's light in life and nature mean that Sikhs should reduce pollution and try for a fair sharing of resources. However, most Sikhs believe the interests of humans should come first.

2.7 The work of a religious organisation in support of conservation

MAIN FACTS

All religions have groups helping to conserve the environment:
- Christian Aid makes sure that its development work protects the environment
- Target Earth is a Christian group which buys up land to re-forest and protect endangered species
- Muslim Aid makes sure that its development work in places like Afghanistan conserves the environment
- the Chipko Movement is a Hindu tree-hugging group founded to prevent trees being cut down.

The reasons why religious organisations work to conserve the environment are the teachings on creation, stewardship and the environment.

The Jewish National Fund

The Jewish National Fund (JNF) is a religious organisation which works in Israel according to the mitzvot of Judaism. Jews from all over the world give donations to the JNF.
The JNF:
- has planted 200 million trees in Israel to reduce the greenhouse effect and to reclaim land from the desert
- has developed a process called 'savannisation' which uses available water to make the desert useful for farming
- has built reservoirs and dams to use the storm water which usually disappears into the desert
- is working to make dangerous places such as landfill sites, waste dumps and old quarries safe and attractive.

In all its work, the Jewish National Fund believes that it is putting into practice the teachings of Judaism about care for the environment:
- Jews believe that the world, and everything in it, was created by God and so is good and sacred. So it must be respected and cared for by humans.
- Judaism teaches that God created humans as his stewards of the Earth to have authority over animals and plants.
- God showed people how to look after the Earth in the mitzvot.
- Life is a test and God will judge Jews on how well they have looked after the world.

KEY FACTS

The Jewish National Fund is a Jewish organisation working for the environment in Israel. It is working to halt desertification, and roll back the desert by savvanisation; as well as dealing with pollution. It does this work because it believes in the Jewish teachings on stewardship and protecting God's creation.

2.8 Animal rights

MAIN FACTS

Most people now agree that animals have a right to be treated humanely. In the United Kingdom, there are many laws forbidding cruelty to animals.

People argue about whether animals have the same rights as humans. If they do, then:

- There should be no medical research done on animals that is not also done on humans.
- There should be no zoos or farms with animals.
- Animals should not be eaten for food.
- Animals should not be hunted, shot, fished, etc.

If animals only have the right not to be made to suffer unnecessarily, then:

- Animals can be used for medical research.
- There can be zoos and farms with animals.
- Animals can be eaten for food.
- Animals can be hunted, but only for food or to remove disease or vermin.

KEY FACTS

There are arguments about whether animals should have the same rights as humans. If they should then they should not be used for food or research. If they only have the right to be treated humanely, then they can be used for food and research.

KEY WORD

Animal rights the belief that animals have rights which should not be exploited by humans.

2.9 Non-religious arguments about animal rights

MAIN FACTS

The arguments for animals having the same rights as humans

- Animals are capable of suffering and of experiencing happiness.
- We give young children rights, but most mature animals are similar to young humans, therefore they should have the same rights.
- There is now evidence from work with apes, chimpanzees and gorillas that some animals are very similar to humans, so they should have the same rights as humans.

Such thinkers argue that animals should not be used by humans for food, nor for medical experiments.

The arguments that animals cannot have the same rights as humans

- To have rights means to be able to use, think and talk about those rights, e.g. the right of freedom of speech means being able to speak. As animals cannot do the things connected with rights, they cannot have them.
- To have rights means being able to choose how to live one's life; and animals are certainly not able to choose how to live their lives.
- There can only be rights for those who are able to protect their rights and no animal can do this.
- Having rights requires living according to laws, but animals live only according to 'the law of the jungle'.

Such thinkers argue that animals should have the right to kind treatment by humans, but they can only have the rights that humans decide they should have.

KEY FACTS

Some people think animals should have the same rights as humans because animals can experience pain and happiness and are at least as advanced as human infants who have rights. Others say animals only have the right to be treated humanely because rights can only be given to those who can respect other people's rights.

2.10 Christian teachings on animal rights

MAIN FACTS

Most Christians believe that animals can be used for medical experiments and should be used for food. However, they also believe that humans should not be cruel to animals and that farmers should care for their animals humanely.

They believe this because:
- God gave humans the right to control animals according to Genesis
- God is the creator of animals as well as humans and the Bible says that humans should respect God's creation.

Some Christians believe that animals should not be used for food or experiments because:
- God is the creator of animals as well as humans and the Bible says that humans should respect God's creation
- it is impossible to use animals for food or experiments without being cruel to them and this is wrong.

KEY FACTS

All Christians believe it is wrong to be cruel to animals. However, some Christians believe animals can be used for food and research because the Bible says humans can rule animals.

Other Christians believe animals should have the same rights as humans because the Bible teaches that Christians should respect God's creation.

2.11 Teachings on animal rights in one non-Christian religion

Islam and animal rights

MAIN FACTS

Muslims believe that animals can be used for medical experiments and should be used for food. However, they also believe that humans should not be cruel to animals and that farmers should care for their animals humanely.

They believe this because:
- the Qur'an says God gave humans the right to control animals
- God is the creator of animals as well as humans and the Qur'an says that animals have feelings and must be dedicated to God when being slaughtered.

KEY FACTS

Muslims believe that animals should be treated kindly but that they can be used for food and research because the Qur'an teaches this.

Judaism and animal rights

MAIN FACTS

Most Jews believe that animals can be used for medical experiments and should be used for food. However, they also believe that humans should not be cruel to animals and that farmers should care for their animals humanely.

They believe this because:
- in Genesis God gave humans the right to control animals
- God created animals, and humans should therefore treat them with respect
- the Torah and Talmud say animals can be used for food, but have strict laws on the humane treatment of animals.

Some Jews believe that animals should not be used for food or experiments because of the laws in the Torah and Talmud about cruelty to animals.

KEY FACTS

All Jews believe it is wrong to be cruel to animals. However, some Jews believe animals can be used for food and research because the Torah says humans can use animals. Other Jews believe animals should have the same rights as humans because the Tenakh teaches that Jews should respect God's creation.

2.11 Teachings on animal rights in one non-Christian religion

Hinduism and animal rights

> **MAIN FACTS**
>
> Most Hindus do not use animals for food or medical experiments. They are vegetarians who believe that cows are sacred and can never be harmed.
> They believe this because:
> - the scriptures teach that the atman is in all living things so that harming animals is like harming God
> - the Law of Manu says that any form of slaughtering is a sin
> - the gods are often shown in animal form
> - in the Gita, Krishna was a vegetarian.
>
> **KEY FACTS**
>
> Most Hindus believe in animal rights and do not believe in using animals for food or research. They believe this because the scriptures teach that Brahman is in all living things, and that the gods often appear as animals.

! Remember
The Law of Manu is an ancient Hindu book teaching how Hindus should live.

Sikhism and animal rights

> **MAIN FACTS**
>
> Sikhs believe that humans should not be cruel to animals. Most Sikhs are vegetarians but some are not.
> However, for those who want to advance on the spiritual path, it is recommended to be vegetarian and therefore be against animal experiments because:
> - Sikhs believe all creation is a part of God
> - the Guru Granth Sahib has many teachings against killing animals
> - causing suffering to animals and birds is to be avoided because the lives of the Gurus are full of stories of their love for animals and birds.
>
> **KEY FACTS**
>
> Most Sikhs believe in animal rights and do not believe in using animals for research because the light of God is in all living things. However, there are different attitudes about using animals for food because the teaching of the Guru Granth Sahib is unclear.

Religion and the Environment 35

PRACTICE QUESTIONS ✓

a What does the word conservation mean? *(2 marks)*
b Choose ONE religion other than Christianity and outline its teaching on creation. *(6 marks)*
c Explain why some Christians are opposed to medical research being carried out on animals. *(8 marks)*
d 'If religious people really cared about the environment, they would stop using cars and washing machines.'
   Do you agree? Give reasons for your opinion, showing you have considered another point of view. In your answer, you should refer to at least one religion. *(4 marks)*

Religion: Peace and Conflict

SECTION 3

3.1 Two areas of conflict in the world today

> **MAIN FACTS**
>
> There are many areas of conflict in the world today and the specification requires you to know of one in detail and one in brief.
>
> ### 1. Israel and Palestine
> There is conflict between Israel and the Palestinian people in the Middle East. The Palestinians want their own Palestinian state in areas which are controlled by Israel. This was partly agreed in the Oslo Agreement (1993–5) but it has still not been put into practice.
>
> The main reasons for the conflict are:
> - The Jews and the Arabs both regard the same area as their homeland.
> - Israel ruled the area from 1000BCE to 132CE and the Palestinians from 635CE to the end of the First World War.
> - Britain captured Palestine during the First World War and promised a homeland for both the Israelis and the Palestinians.
> - Many Jews came to the area to escape the Nazis in Germany during the 1930s and 1940s and after they revolted against the British, they established the State of Israel in 1947 which was recognised by the United Nations, but not by the Palestinians.
> - Israel occupied the rest of Palestine after a war in 1967.
> - The Palestinians want their land back, but Israel will only give it back if the Palestinians accept the existence of Israel.
>
> ### 2. Kashmir
> Kashmir is a large area between the North of India and the East of Pakistan, it has been fought over since the British left India in 1947. Both India and Pakistan claim the area and a full-scale war could break out between these countries at any time.
>
> The main reasons for this conflict are:
> - When Britain left India in 1947 the majority Muslim areas of the North did not join India but became the Muslim state of West Pakistan and East Pakistan (now Bangladesh).

KEY WORD

World peace the basic aim of the United Nations by removing the causes of war.

- Kashmir was majority Muslim, but did not join Pakistan because the ruler of Kashmir was Hindu and there were a lot of Hindus in Kashmir.
- Ever since Pakistan, and Muslim Kashmiri rebels, have been fighting to make Kashmir an independent Muslim state.

KEY FACTS

Conflict in the world today means groups of people fighting each other. Conflict is happening in Israel/Palestine over establishing separate Palestinian and Israeli states. Conflict is happening in Kashmir because the Hindus want to continue being ruled by India, and the Muslims want to be ruled by Pakistan.

3.2 Nuclear weapons and other weapons of mass destruction

MAIN FACTS

Weapons of mass destruction are weapons which can kill thousands, if not hundreds of thousands, of people in one strike. There are three types of WMD:

1. Nuclear weapons

Nuclear weapons were first produced towards the end of the Second World War. In 1945, the Americans dropped an atom bomb on Hiroshima, killing 84,000 people, and Nagasaki. Since then, defence scientists have developed nuclear weapons further and the hydrogen bomb is 1,000 times more powerful than the atom bombs dropped on Japan.

Nuclear weapons have the potential to destroy the Earth and many people believe that there have been no world wars since 1945 because when two countries have nuclear weapons, they will hesitate to attack each other, because the other country could destroy them. This is known as MAD (mutually assured destruction). Only the United States, Russia, United Kingdom, France, China, India and Pakistan definitely have nuclear weapons, but Israel may also have them.

2. Biological weapons

Biological agents can potentially kill as many people as nuclear weapons, though they act more slowly than chemical or nuclear weapons and are difficult to deliver effectively. An example of a biological weapon is the bacteria that causes the disease anthrax which usually results in toxic shock and death.

KEY WORDS

Nuclear weapons weapons based on atomic fission or fusion.

Other weapons of mass destruction non-nuclear weapons that can destroy large areas and/or large numbers of people, e.g. chemical weapons.

3. Chemical weapons

Chemical weapons are such things as nerve gas, or poison gas as used in the First World War. They injure, or kill, by affecting the skin, eyes, lungs, blood, nerves, or other organs.

The major problem with weapons of mass destruction is that they deliberately target innocent civilians including children, the old and women. Can it ever be religiously or morally right to use such weapons?

KEY FACTS

Nuclear weapons use nuclear fission or fusion to create mass destruction. Biological weapons use diseases to create mass destruction. Chemical weapons use special chemicals to create mass destruction.

3.3 Christian attitudes to pacifism

MAIN FACTS

For the first 300 years of Christianity, Christians refused to fight in wars. So today, some Christians believe that war is so wrong that Christians should never fight in wars. They are called Christian pacifists. There are many Christian pacifist groups such as the Roman Catholic Pax Christi. The Quakers, the Plymouth Brethren and the Christadelphians are Churches whose members have to be pacifists.

Christian pacifists believe they should not fight in wars because:

- Jesus said Christians should love their enemies and turn the other cheek when attacked
- the fifth commandment says, 'Do not kill'
- Jesus would not let Peter fight back when Jesus was being arrested
- horrible things happen to innocent civilians in modern wars
- they believe that peace can only come when people refuse to fight.

KEY FACTS

Some Christians believe that they should work for peace by refusing to fight in wars. They believe Christians should be pacifists because Jesus taught Christians to love their enemies.

KEY WORD

Pacifism refusing to fight in wars.

Religion: Peace and Conflict

3.4 Christian attitudes to 'just war'

MAIN FACTS

Most Christian Churches believe that fighting wars can be the best way of bringing peace as long as the war is a just one. A 'just war' is one which:
- is fought in self-defence against an attacker or to remove great unfairness
- is only fought after all ways of trying to solve the problem without war have been tried
- uses fair methods
- does not harm civilians.

Most Christians believe in fighting just wars because:
- St Augustine and St Thomas Aquinas said Christians could fight in just wars
- Jesus did not condemn soldiers, he actually praised the faith of a Roman centurion
- St Paul said Christians should obey the orders of the state
- if we need a police force to protect innocent people against criminals, we need armed forces to protect innocent states against criminal ones.

KEY FACTS

Some Christians believe that the way to bring peace is to be prepared to fight in 'just wars'. They will fight to defend the weak and to bring peace to the world because this has always been the Church's teaching.

KEY WORD

'Just War' a war that is fought for the right reasons and in a right way.

'Just war' = a war for the right reasons and in the right way.

3.5 The attitudes to war of one non-Christian religion

Islam and attitudes to war

MAIN FACTS

Peace is the ideal for all Muslims as one of the meanings of the word Islam is 'peace'. However, Islam teaches that Muslims should fight if Islam is being attacked or if people are suffering injustice. They believe, though, that war must be a last resort when all other options to solve the problem have been tried and that the war must be fought in a just way so that the minimum amount of suffering is caused and innocent civilians are not involved.

Muslims believe that this type of war is a struggle for God (jihad) because:
- the Qur'an says that Muslims must fight if they are attacked
- Muhammad fought in wars
- there are many hadith from Muhammad saying Muslims should fight in just wars
- the Qur'an says that Muslims dying in jihad will go straight to heaven.

KEY FACTS

Muslims believe in peace, but Islam teaches that if the faith is attacked, Muslims must defend their faith by fighting jihad (a just war fought in a just way). They believe this because it is taught in the Qur'an.

Judaism and attitudes to war

MAIN FACTS

Peace is the ideal state for all Jews. The Jewish word for 'hello' translates as 'peace be with you'. However, Judaism expects Jews to fight if they are attacked by an enemy, if they are asked to aid a country that is being attacked, and if all other attempts to resolve the conflict have failed.

Jews believe they can fight in wars because:
- there are mitzvot saying that Jews must fight when attacked
- there are many accounts in the Tenakh of how Israel had to fight wars to preserve her independence
- the Holocaust reminds Jews what can happen if there is no army to defend Jews against attack.

However, there are some Jewish pacifists who believe that war is wrong in the modern world because modern weapons are bound to harm so many innocent people.

3.5 The attitudes to war of one non-Christian religion

KEY FACTS

Jews believe in peace, but Judaism teaches that Jews must defend themselves if they are attacked, as stated in the Torah and Talmud. However, some Jews are pacifists because they think modern weapons are too horrible ever to be used.

Hinduism and attitudes to war

MAIN FACTS

Although Hinduism is dedicated to peace, there are different attitudes to war among Hindus.

Some Hindus believe that violence in any form is wrong and that Hindus should be able to struggle for justice without going to war. They believe this because:
- the Hindu belief of ahimsa means non-violence
- killing people puts a person's soul further from moksha
- Gandhi's struggle for Indian independence from the British showed pacifism can work as a way of removing injustice.

Many Hindus believe that it is right to fight in wars in order to resist attack or to remove great injustice. They believe this because:
- the second Hindu caste is the warrior caste, whose duty (karma) is to defend Hinduism
- the Bhagavad Gita says that Hindus must fight in just wars, as killing people does not kill their souls
- there are many stories in the Hindu Scriptures of Hindu gods being involved in wars during their avatars on Earth.

KEY FACTS

All Hindus believe in peace, but there are different attitudes to war in Hinduism:
- Some Hindus will not take part in any wars because they believe they should follow ahimsa (non-violence).
- Some Hindus think it is right to fight if attacked because this is taught in scriptures such as the Bhagavad Gita.

Remember
Moksha means salvation, when the soul is so pure it is not reborn after death.

3.5 The attitudes to war of one non-Christian religion

Sikhism and attitudes to war

MAIN FACTS

Although Sikhs are strongly in favour of peace, they are expected to fight wars against oppression and injustice.

The Sikh idea of the just war is called 'Dharam Yudh', meaning 'war in the defence of what is right'.

In Sikhism a war is a just war if:
- all other ways of ending the conflict have been tried
- the motive is justice, not revenge or hatred
- only the minimum force needed for success is used
- civilians are not harmed and places of worship (of any faith) not damaged
- treaties and cease-fires must be honoured
- soldiers who surrender should not be harmed.

The main difference from other just war theories is that Sikhs believe that if a war is just it should be fought even if it cannot be won.

KEY FACTS

Sikhs are not pacifists and are expected to fight to protect the oppressed and human rights. However, the war must be fought justly. 'Just wars' must be fought by Sikhs, even if there is no chance of success.

3.6 The work of a religious organisation for world peace

MAIN FACTS

Pax Christi is a Roman Catholic group dedicated to peace and non-violence. Pax Christi USA was founded in 1972 and is dedicated to:
- reflecting the peace of Christ (*pax Christi*) in the lives of American people
- witnessing the call of Christians to non-violence.

The work of Pax Christi:
- publicly condemning such things as the invasion of Iraq
- organising public debates on the morality of nuclear weapons
- criticising the American government's defence policy
- working to remove the economic and racial causes of war.

Reasons why Pax Christi does the work:
- Jesus said Christians should love their enemies and turn the other cheek when attacked
- Jesus would not let Peter fight back when Jesus was being arrested
- horrible things happen to innocent civilians in modern wars.

KEY FACTS

Pax Christi USA is the American branch of a Catholic Christian group working for world peace. Pax Christi USA is trying to persuade the American government to give up its nuclear weapons and work for world peace.

44 Religion: Peace and Conflict

3.7 The nature of bullying

MAIN FACTS

School bullying can include:
- being called names
- being pinched, kicked or hit
- having possessions taken
- being ignored or left out
- receiving abusive texts or e-mails.

Such school bullying can result in poor exam results, injury, mental illness, suicide or murder.

Childline, a free, confidential phone line for children experiencing problems, says bullying is the single biggest problem facing children today.

Other forms of bullying can take place among adults. Managers or supervisors at work can use their power and authority to frighten or humiliate workers who are under their control.

KEY FACTS

Bullying is when stronger people pick on weak people to make their lives miserable. Bullying can lead to stress, nervous breakdown or even suicide.

KEY WORD

Bullying intimidating/frightening people weaker than yourself.

3.8 Non-religious attitudes to bullying

MAIN FACTS

Bullying is not approved of by society and the law tries to protect the victims of bullying.
- All schools must have an anti-bullying policy.
- All trade unions have procedures to help and protect workers who are being bullied at work.
- The law treats verbal bullying as assault and any bullying with physical injury as aggravated assault, both of which carry prison sentences.

Society disapproves of bullying because:
- in a democracy, everyone has the right to be able to live free from fear
- bullying has harmful effects on society as people who are bullied will not be able to do the work they are capable of.

A civilised society is based on people respecting each other and obeying the law. Clearly, bullies break the law and have no respect for the people they bully.

KEY FACTS

Non-religious people are against bullying because it harms people and harms society. The law punishes bullies because they deny people their rights.

3.9 Religious attitudes to bullying

MAIN FACTS

All religions see bullying as wrong because they:
- see using violence without a just cause as sinful, and bullying always involves unjust violence
- see human beings as a creation of God – bullying is mistreating God's creation
- teach that it is the duty of religious people to protect the weak and innocent
- teach that harming other people will bring bad results in your life after death.

KEY FACTS

Religious people are against bullying because all religions teach it is wrong. All holy books teach that people have a duty to protect the innocent and respect other people.

3.10 Conflicts between family and friends

MAIN FACTS

Conflict does not only occur in wars or bullying. Conflict with friends or family can have terrible effects on people's lives. Friendship can break up, wives or husbands can be battered, people in the family can refuse to have anything to do with each other etc.

Some family conflicts you could use in the examination might include:
- parents refusing to accept a child's choice of partner because of their religion, race, class etc.
- brothers and sisters disagreeing over the care of their elderly parents
- children's choice of career (e.g. wanting to be a priest (minister), imam or charity worker) after their parents have spent a lot of money on their university education
- conflicts between husband and wife about children, money, affairs etc.
- disagreements over the contents of wills
- quarrels over religious and moral issues e.g. a child deciding to cohabit rather than marry.

Some causes of conflicts between friends you could use in the examination:
- jealousy because one friend is more successful than another e.g. someone wins the lottery and refuses to share their winnings with their friends
- jealousy over boyfriends/girlfriends
- quarrels over moral and religious issues e.g. a Catholic girl wanting an abortion, a Muslim boy dating a Christian girl.

KEY FACTS

Conflicts can happen in families or between friends. They happen because people do not accept friends or family members having different ideas or being more successful.

3.11 Christian teachings on forgiveness and reconciliation

MAIN FACTS

Christians believe that it is their duty to try to bring reconciliation between families and friends who are in conflict and that it is a Christian's duty to forgive those who attack them. They believe this because:
- Jesus died on the cross to bring reconciliation and forgiveness
- Jesus told Peter to forgive his brother up to 77 times
- Jesus said that if Christians do not forgive others, they will not be forgiven themselves
- St Paul said that Christians should try to live in peace with everyone.

Nevertheless, Christians believe that a conflict about morality or religion would not be resolvable if, for example, the children were following Christian teachings and the parents were not.

KEY FACTS

Christians believe they should try to settle conflicts between families and friends. They believe they should forgive those who attack them. Christians believe they should do this because of the teachings of Jesus.

KEY WORDS

Forgiveness the act of stopping the blaming of someone and/or pardoning them for what they have done wrong.

Reconciliation bringing together people who were opposed to each other.

3.12 Teachings on forgiveness and reconciliation in one non-Christian religion

Islam: forgiveness and reconciliation

MAIN FACTS

Islam teaches that Muslims should try to resolve conflicts and should be forgiving to those who cause them offence. They believe this because:
- God is compassionate and merciful to sinners, so Muslims should also be forgiving.
- How can Muslims ask for God's forgiveness on the Last Day if *they* are not prepared to forgive people?
- The Qur'an says that Muslims should forgive those who offend them.
- Muhammad said in many hadiths that Muslims should be forgiving.

Nevertheless, Muslims believe that a conflict about morality or religion would not be resolvable if, for example, the children were following Islamic teachings and the parents were not.

KEY FACTS

Muslims try to forgive those who wrong them and try to resolve conflicts because this is the teaching of the Qur'an. Muslims are taught to forgive if they expect God to forgive them.

Remember
Hadiths are sayings or actions of the Prophet Muhammad.

3.12 Teachings on forgiveness and reconciliation in one non-Christian religion

Judaism: forgiveness and reconciliation

MAIN FACTS

Judaism teaches that Jews should forgive those who wrong them, and the days between Rosh Hashanah and Yom Kippur are dedicated to resolving any conflicts that may have arisen with families or friends over the past year.ABmove Jews believe in forgiveness because:
- the Tenakh teaches that God forgives those who turn to him in repentance
- the Tenakh teaches that Jews should forgive those who wrong them
- the rabbis encourage Jews to forgive those who wrong them
- it is Jewish belief that Jews should forgive those who have wronged them when on their deathbed so that God will forgive their sins.

Nevertheless, Jews believe that a conflict about morality or religion would not be resolvable if, for example, the children were following Jewish teachings and the parents were not.

KEY FACTS

Jews believe they should forgive those who wrong them because it is taught in the Tenakh. They also believe it is their duty to resolve conflicts as every year they have Yom Kippur when they must forgive people and resolve any personal conflicts.

Remember
Yom Kippur is the Day of Atonement.

3.12 Teachings on forgiveness and reconciliation in one non-Christian religion

Hinduism: forgiveness and reconciliation

MAIN FACTS

There are differences among Hindus in their attitudes to forgiveness.

Some Hindus do not believe in forgiveness because:
- they believe that everything is a result of karma and nothing should be done to change people's karma.

Most Hindus believe in forgiveness because:
- it is better for one's soul to forgive those who have committed wrong
- in the gunas, forgiveness is a quality of light which leads the soul to moksha
- the Upanishads teach that it is dangerous for the soul not to forgive
- many swamis believe that forgiveness is a part of moksha.

KEY FACTS

All Hindus believe they should try to bring reconciliation to conflicts to gain good karma. However:
- some Hindus think the law of cause and effect (karma) means no forgiveness
- others believe that forgiving others is the way to moksha.

Remember

Karma is the law of cause and effect – what we do affects what we are reborn as.

3.12 Teachings on forgiveness and reconciliation in one non-Christian religion

Sikhism: forgiveness and reconciliation

> **MAIN FACTS**
>
> Sikhism began because Guru Nanak wanted to reconcile the religions of Islam and Hinduism that divided India. Sikhs are taught to forgive as a way of reconciling conflict.
>
> Sikhs believe in forgiveness and reconciliation because:
> - There are many examples of the Gurus showing forgiveness and seeking reconciliation.
> - The Guru Granth Sahib teaches the importance of forgiveness and reconciliation.
> - The festival of Paryushana Parva celebrates friendship and forgiveness.
>
> Nevertheless, Sikhs believe that a conflict over moral or religious issues would not be able to be resolved e.g. if Sikhs were criticising the khalsa.
>
> **KEY FACTS**
>
> Sikhism believes in forgiveness and reconciliation wherever possible because this was the teaching and example of the Gurus. Sikhism has always tried to reconcile the conflicts raised between Hindus and Muslims in India.

PRACTICE QUESTIONS ✓

a What does the word pacifism mean? *(2 marks)*

b Outline different attitudes to war in Christianity. *(6 marks)*

c Choose ONE area of conflict in the world and explain why the conflict is happening. *(8 marks)*

d 'Religious people should never argue with their families.'
Do you agree? Give reasons for your opinion, showing you have considered another point of view. In your answer, you should refer to at least one religion. *(4 marks)*

Religion: Crime and Punishment

SECTION 4

4.1 The differences between sin and crime

MAIN FACTS

A sin is an act against the will of God. A crime is an act that breaks the law of the land. Many crimes are also sins, e.g. stealing, murder and rape are crimes *and* break religious laws.

However, sins are not always crimes:
- If a millionaire is asked for food by a starving man and he refuses to give him anything, he has not committed a crime, but he would have broken the laws of God.
- If a man has sex with a married woman, he is committing a sin, but adultery is not a crime.

In the same way, crimes are not always sins:
- Martin Luther King committed crimes in his fight for civil rights for black Americans (e.g. sitting on a bus seat reserved for whites) but these were not sins.
- Germans who gave jobs to Jews during the Nazi rule were committing a crime, but it was not a sin.

KEY FACTS

Breaking God's laws is a sin, breaking society's laws is a crime. Often wrong actions are both a sin and a crime, but many sins, like adultery, are not crimes, and unjust laws are not sins.

KEY WORDS

Sin an act against the will of God.

Crime an act against the law.

4.2 The need for law and justice

MAIN FACTS

Laws are rules about how people are expected to behave. The courts and the police make sure that all members of society obey the law.

Justice means rewarding the good and punishing the bad and making sure that what is right happens in society.

Society needs laws so that:
- people know what sort of behaviour to expect from each other
- people are protected from violence
- people can be protected from someone taking what they have worked for.

Why does there need to be a connection between the law and justice?

- If a law is unjust people will feel that it is right to break the law.
- If a law does not give justice to people, people will take the law into their own hands.

To achieve justice, the United Kingdom has a Legal Aid system which uses taxes to give free legal help to poor people.

KEY FACTS

Laws tell people how to behave, and justice makes sure the good are rewarded and the evil punished. Society needs laws for it to work properly, and the laws need to be just.

KEY WORDS

Law rules made by Parliament and enforceable by the courts.

Justice due allocation of reward and punishment, the maintenance of what is right.

4.3 Christian attitudes to justice

MAIN FACTS

Christians believe that the world should be ruled justly and that God will reward the good and punish the bad. They believe that they should:
- work for justice and so they campaign for the cancelling of Third World debt (e.g. Jubilee 2000)
- work to improve life in Less Economically Developed Countries (LEDCs) (e.g. Christian Aid)
- work for poor people in the United Kingdom (e.g. the Salvation Army).

Christians believe in justice because:
- the Bible says that God is a God of justice
- the Bible says that people should be treated fairly
- Jesus said that the rich should share with the poor
- there are many statements in the New Testament about treating people fairly and equally
- the Churches have made statements about the need for Christians to work for justice in the world.

KEY FACTS

Christians believe in justice because the Bible says God is a God of justice who will reward the good and punish the bad at the end of the world. Christians work for justice by campaigning for fair treatment of the poor etc.

Jubilee 2000 = a Christian campaign to get rich governments and banks to cancel the debts of poor countries.

Religion: Crime and Punishment 55

4.4 The attitudes to justice of one non-Christian religion

Islam and justice

MAIN FACTS

Muslims believe that the world should be ruled justly and that God will reward the good and punish the bad. They believe that the laws of the world should be the law of God (Shari'ah). Muslims believe that all people should have equal rights and as part of their belief in justice they work for a fairer share of resources for LEDCs through groups such as Muslim Aid and through the pillar of zakah and refusing to be involved in charging or receiving interest.

They believe this because:
- the Qur'an says God is just
- the Qur'an says that Muslims should treat people fairly
- Muslims believe it is part of their role as stewards of God's creation to treat all people fairly
- the Shari'ah is based on justice for everyone, with everyone being treated equally.

KEY FACTS

Muslims believe in justice because the Qur'an says that God is just. Muslims believe they must work for justice through zakah/zakat and the Shari'ah.

Remember
Zakah (or zakat) is the pillar of Islam which makes rich people pay two and a half per cent of their wealth to help the poor.

Judaism and justice

MAIN FACTS

Jews believe that justice is very important and that God wants the world to be ruled justly. They believe that all people should have equal rights. As part of their belief in justice, many Jews work for equal rights and a fairer sharing of resources, by helping groups such as Oxfam.

They believe this because:
- the Torah says that God is a God of Justice
- the Tenakh says that all people should be treated fairly
- the Tenakh, Talmud and rabbis say that the rich should share with the poor
- there are many statements in the Responsa about how Jews should treat all people fairly and equally.

KEY FACTS

Jews believe in justice because the Torah says God is a God of justice. Jews work for justice by working for fairer shares for the poor.

Remember
The Responsa are decisions of rabbis about how Jews should live.

4.4 The attitudes to justice of one non-Christian religion

Hinduism and justice

> **MAIN FACTS**
>
> The Hindu idea of justice is based on dharma. For most Hindus this means that they should try to make the world a place of justice. They do this by treating all people as equals, working for equal rights and a fairer sharing of the Earth's resources.
> They believe this because:
> - the Hindu goal is to gain moksha and this means fulfilling the dharma and working for justice
> - the Hindu scriptures encourage Hindus to work for justice
> - great Hindu leaders such as Gandhi spent their lives working for justice
> - Hindu Gurus and swamis teach that treating people justly improves the soul.
>
> Some Hindus believe that justice comes through operating the caste system correctly. They believe this because:
> - the caste system rewards the good for their past lives
> - the caste system punishes the bad for their past lives.
>
> **KEY FACTS**
>
> All Hindus believe in justice based on dharma, but:
> - many Hindus believe they should work for justice because this cleanses their soul so they can gain moksha
> - some Hindus believe the caste system gives justice by rewarding the good and punishing the bad.

Remember
Dharma is the religious duty of Hindus – how they must live to gain moksha (freedom from rebirth).

Sikhism and justice

> **MAIN FACTS**
>
> Sikhs believe God is just and the justice of God is perfect. Sikhs think it is the right of people to get justice, and so it is the duty of Sikhs to bring God's justice into the world.
> Human justice often gives better treatment to the rich and powerful who can sometimes escape punishment. Sikhs believe this is wrong and that God's justice is better.
> Sikhs believe in justice because:
> - the Guru Granth Sahib teaches that God Himself is just
> - Sikhism teaches that at the end of people's lives, God will do full justice to everyone
> - the Guru Granth Sahib teaches that there should be justice for all human beings
> - all the Gurus worked for justice and Sikhs should follow their example.

4.4 The attitudes to justice of one non-Christian religion

KEY FACTS

Sikhism teaches that God is just and justice comes from God. It is the duty of Sikhs to work for justice and remove injustice. Sikhs believe in justice because it is taught in the Guru Granth Sahib and all the Gurus worked for justice.

4.5 Theories of punishment

MAIN FACTS

In order to have justice and make sure laws are obeyed, society has law courts and punishments. Punishment of criminals is based on these theories:
- retribution – the idea that criminals should pay for their crimes
- deterrence – the idea that if punishments are severe enough, people will be frightened of committing crimes
- reform – the idea that people who commit crimes need to be shown why it is wrong and be helped to lead crime-free lives
- protection – the idea that punishment should be used to protect society from criminals who cannot be reformed.

KEY FACTS

The law uses punishment to bring justice to society. A theory of punishment means an idea of what punishment should be trying to do to the criminal. The main theories are: retribution, deterrence, reformation and protection.

KEY WORDS

Deterrence the idea that punishments should be of such a nature that they will put people off committing crimes.

Punishment a penalty given for any crime or offence.

Reform the idea that punishments should try to change criminals so they will not commit crimes again.

Retribution the idea that punishments should make criminals pay for what they have done wrong.

4.6 Christianity and punishment

MAIN FACTS

Some Christians believe that the only purpose of punishment is to reform the criminal. Everyone can be saved and criminals should be given the chance to repent and change their lives.
They believe this because:
- Jesus said Christians should not judge others
- Christianity is about the power of God to save people and change their lives
- the Church has always seen itself as a way to bring new life to criminals
- the Churches have made many statements about the need for punishment to be used to reform criminals so that they can live in society.

Some Christians believe that punishment should be used to deter criminals and to protect society as well as reform criminals. They believe this because:
- St Paul said magistrates should uphold the law
- without a police force and punishment for criminals, society would collapse
- the Churches have made statements that punishment can be used to deter and protect
- Jesus punished the money changers when he threw them out of the Temple.

KEY FACTS

There are two Christians attitudes to punishment:
1. Some Christians believe only in reform because Christians should not judge others.
2. Some Christians believe in deterrence and protection as well as reform because of the teachings of St Paul.

4.7 One non-Christian religion and punishment

Islam and punishment

MAIN FACTS

Islam teaches that criminals should be punished and the Qur'an sets down specific punishments for some crimes. Islam teaches that punishment should be based on deterrence and reform. Some crimes are punished by the criminal paying compensation.

Muslims believe that punishment should be based on deterrence, retribution and reform because:

- It is what the Qur'an teaches:
  - punishing by whipping, amputation and compensation allows the criminal to stay in society with their family, where it is believed they are less likely to reoffend
  - severe punishments are a deterrent but are only used as a last resort.
- The Shari'ah makes sure that the punishment is only given to the guilty.

KEY FACTS

Islam teaches that punishment should be used to deter and reform, and to make criminals pay for what they have done (retribution) because this is taught in the Qur'an.

Judaism and punishment

MAIN FACTS

Jews believe that society has a right to punish criminals. They believe that the reasons for punishment are deterrence, protection and retribution. However, they also see that there should be some reform, as successful reform of criminals is a way of protecting society from future crimes.

They believe this because:

- the Torah says that criminals should be punished
- the Torah gives deterrence, protection and retribution as the reasons for punishment
- society would collapse if criminals were not punished
- rabbis have always been involved in the Jewish court system.

KEY FACTS

Judaism teaches that punishment should be used to deter and reform criminals and to make criminals pay for what they have done (retribution) because this is taught in the Torah.

4.7 One non-Christian religion and punishment

Hinduism and punishment

> **MAIN FACTS**
>
> Hindus believe that it is part of the dharma of rulers to punish those who break the law. Hindus believe that punishment should be used to deter and reform criminals so that society is protected from future crime. They also believe in retribution so that criminals pay for what they have done. They believe this because:
> - the Vedas and Upanishads say that crimes must be punished
> - other Hindu scriptures give guidelines on punishments
> - the Mahabharata says that a ruler has a duty to punish criminals
> - the law of karma is based on retribution.
>
> **KEY FACTS**
>
> Hindus believe that punishment should be used for reform, deterrence, protection and retribution because this is the teaching of the holy books and the law of karma.

Sikhism and punishment

> **MAIN FACTS**
>
> Sikhs are taught that it is the duty of rulers to uphold the law and punish those who break the law. Sikhism teaches that punishment should protect society from criminals, deter people from committing crimes and reform those who have committed crimes. Sikhs believe in punishment because:
> - the Gurus and the Guru Granth Sahib teach that the law must protect the weak
> - the Rahit Maryada suggests prison sentences for crimes
> - the Gurus said that punishment should help criminals to reform rather than be for retribution and retaliation
> - deterrence, protection and reform are the only punishments which allow Sikhs to consider others.
>
> **KEY FACTS**
>
> Sikhs believe that punishment should be used for reform, deterrence and protection because this is the teaching of the Gurus, the Guru Granth Sahib and the Rahit Maryada.

4.8 A religious prisoner of conscience

MAIN FACTS

You have to study a prisoner of conscience – someone who has not committed any crimes who has been imprisoned for their religious beliefs. The prisoner can be from the twentieth or twenty-first centuries. A prisoner of conscience from the time of the Nazis and the Second World War was Dietrich Bonhoeffer.

Bonhoeffer was a Christian pacifist and a lecturer in Christianity at Berlin University. When Hitler came to power, Bonhoeffer criticised him in radio broadcasts and in lectures. Bonhoeffer was banned from teaching in Germany and became pastor of two German Lutheran churches in London. Whilst in London he tried to tell the British the truth about Hitler. In 1935, Bonhoeffer returned to Germany to train pastors who were against Hitler and he was arrested in 1937.

Reasons for the arrest

- He had made statements saying that Christians should not obey the Nazi laws on the Jews.
- He said that Christians should refuse to do military service for the Nazis.
- He had preached sermons in Berlin saying that Christians should not obey laws which were against Christian principles.

His arrest made Bonhoeffer realise that pacifism could not work with the Nazis and he decided that it was his Christian duty to join the German movement which was trying to overthrow Hitler and the Nazis. Bonhoeffer was involved in plots to kill Hitler and after the July Bomb Plot failed in July 1944, he was arrested again and executed at Flossenberg extermination camp in April 1945, just before the war ended.

KEY FACTS

Dietrich Bonhoeffer was a German Christian who was arrested by the Nazis in 1937 because he had told Christians not to support Hitler. After his release, he joined plots to kill Hitler and was executed just before the Second World War ended.

4.9 The nature of capital punishment

MAIN FACTS

Capital punishment is a punishment that takes away the life of the criminal. It is also called execution or the death penalty. Capital punishment has not been used in the United Kingdom since 1970.

Non-religious arguments in favour of capital punishment

- If people know that committing murder will lead to their execution, they will not murder.
- If murderers are executed, they are no longer a threat to society.
- The only punishment to fit the crime of taking a life is to take the murderer's life.

Non-religious arguments against capital punishment

- Courts do convict innocent people and nothing can be done to release an innocent person who has been executed.
- Statistics show that countries that do not use the death penalty have a lower murder rate than those that do.
- Murderers do not expect to be caught when they commit their murders.
- Murderers sometimes try to commit suicide when they are serving life imprisonment, so prison must be a worse sentence than death.

KEY FACTS

Capital punishment is punishment that takes the life of the criminal. Some people think it is a good idea because it takes a life for a life and deters people from murdering others. Some people think it is a bad punishment because there is evidence that it does not deter, and mistakes in trials can lead to innocent people being killed for crimes they did not commit.

KEY WORD

Capital punishment the death penalty for a crime or offence.

4.10 Christian attitudes to capital punishment

MAIN FACTS

Many Christians believe that capital punishment is un-Christian. They believe this because:
- Jesus came to save (reform) sinners, but you cannot reform a dead person
- Jesus said that an eye for an eye and a tooth for a tooth is wrong for Christians
- Christianity teaches that all life is sacred, if abortion and euthanasia are wrong, so is capital punishment
- they also believe all the non-religious arguments against capital punishment.

Other Christians believe that capital punishment can be used to prevent murder and keep order in society. They believe this because:
- the Old Testament gives the death penalty as the punishment for various offences
- the Roman Catholic Church and the Church of England have not cancelled their statements that capital punishment can be used by the state
- Christian thinkers such as Aquinas said that the protection of society is a more important part of punishment than the reform of the criminal
- they would also use all the non-religious arguments in favour of capital punishment.

KEY FACTS

There are two Christian attitudes to capital punishment:
1. Many Christians think capital punishment is wrong because of the teachings of Jesus.
2. Some Christians agree with capital punishment to keep order in society because it is the teaching of the Church.

4.11 The attitudes of one non-Christian religion to capital punishment

Islam and capital punishment

MAIN FACTS

Most Muslims agree with capital punishment because:
- the Qur'an says that death is the punishment for murder, adultery and denying Islam
- Muhammad made several statements agreeing with capital punishment
- Muhammad sentenced people to death when he was ruler of Madinah
- the Shari'ah says that death is the punishment for murder and adultery
- they would also agree with all the non-religious arguments in favour of capital punishment.

Some Muslims disagree with capital punishment because of the non-religious arguments against it and because the Shari'ah allows compensation to be paid to the family of a murder victim rather than capital punishment.

KEY FACTS

Most Muslims agree with capital punishment because it is the punishment for certain crimes stated in the Qur'an. Some Muslims do not agree with capital punishment because it is not stated as compulsory in the Shari'ah, and for non-religious reasons.

Judaism and capital punishment

MAIN FACTS

Most Jews agree with capital punishment, but only if there is no possibility of reforming the murderer. They believe this because:
- the Torah says that capital punishment should be used for certain crimes
- the Talmud says that capital punishment can be used, but with many restrictions. The basis of punishment is the protection of society, and therefore murderers, who will always be a danger to society, should be executed
- they would also use the non-religious arguments in favour of capital punishment.

Some Jews do not agree with capital punishment because of the teachings of the Mishnah and the non-religious arguments against capital punishment.

Remember
The Mishnah is the writings of the Oral Torah and is the basis of the Talmud.

4.11 The attitudes of one non-Christian religion to capital punishment

> **KEY FACTS**
>
> Most Jews agree with capital punishment because it is approved of by the Torah, and they think it will deter criminals. Some Jews think capital punishment is wrong because of what the Mishnah says.

Hinduism and capital punishment

> **MAIN FACTS**
>
> Most Hindus agree with capital punishment for murderers. They believe this because:
> - the Vedas say that ahimsa does not apply to criminals
> - the Law of Manu says that a Hindu can kill someone to maintain social order
> - the Vahara Purana says that a king can execute criminals to restore the correct dharma
> - they would also use the non-religious arguments in favour of capital punishment.
>
> Some Hindus do not agree with capital punishment because of Gandhi's teachings and the non-religious arguments against capital punishment.
>
> **KEY FACTS**
>
> Most Hindus believe capital punishment should be used for murderers because that is the teaching of the Law of Manu. Some Hindus disagree with capital punishment because of the teachings of Gandhi and non-religious arguments.

4.11 The attitudes of one non-Christian religion to capital punishment

Sikhism and capital punishment

MAIN FACTS

Most Sikhs are opposed to capital punishment and think it should only be used in the most extreme cases. Executing a prisoner is 'killing in cold blood' which can never be justified in Sikhism.

Most Sikhs are opposed to capital punishment because:
- there are no clear instructions on capital punishment in the Guru Granth Sahib
- the Ten Gurus appear to have been against capital punishment
- killing in cold blood is banned by Sikhism.

Some Sikhs agree with capital punishment for non-religious reasons.

KEY FACTS

Most Sikhs are opposed to capital punishment because there are Sikh teachings against killing in cold blood. Some Sikhs agree with capital punishment because there are no clear instructions in the scriptures.

PRACTICE QUESTIONS ✓

a Name TWO theories of punishment. *(2 marks)*

b Outline Christian teaching on forgiveness. *(6 marks)*

c Choose ONE religion other than Christianity and explain why there are different attitudes to capital punishment among its followers. *(8 marks)*

d 'Committing a sin is as bad as committing a crime.'
Do you agree? Give reasons for your opinion, showing you have considered another point of view. In your answer, you should refer to at least one religion. *(4 marks)*

SECTION 5.1 Religion and Medical Issues

5.1.1 Medical treatments for infertility

> ### MAIN FACTS
>
> Medical technology now allows the following treatments for infertile couples:
>
> **In-vitro-fertilisation (IVF)** – an egg is taken from the woman's womb, fertilised in a laboratory and put back in the womb.
>
> **Artificial Insemination by Husband (AIH)** – the man's sperm is put into the woman's womb by medical means.
>
> **Artificial Insemination by Donor (AID)** – an unknown man's (donor's) sperm is put into the woman's womb by medical means.
>
> **Egg donation** – an unknown woman's (donor's) egg and the man's sperm are fertilised by IVF and put into the woman's womb.
>
> **Embryo donation** – when both sperm and egg are from unknown donors and are fertilised by IVF then placed in the wife's womb.
>
> **Surrogacy** – the egg and sperm of the man and woman, or the egg or sperm of the man or woman and an unknown donor's sperm or egg, are fertilised by IVF and then placed in another woman's womb and the baby handed to the couple after the birth.
>
> These medical treatments are supervised by the Human Fertilisation and Embryology Authority, but many are not available on the NHS.
>
> ### Non-religious arguments about fertility treatments
>
> Most non-religious people support couples' rights to fertility treatments and do not have any problems with most of the treatments. Some people do have concerns such as:
> - the psychological problems of a surrogate mother giving up the baby
> - children not knowing their genetic parents if a donor is used.
>
> However, from 1 April 2005, children born from these treatments using a donor have the right to know who the donor was.

KEY FACTS

Infertility is when a couple cannot have a baby. There are now several medical treatments that can help infertile couples to have babies: IVF, artificial insemination, egg and embryo donation.

5.1.2 Christian attitudes to infertility treatments

MAIN FACTS

There are two Christian attitudes to infertility treatments:
1. Roman Catholics and some other Christians ban all forms of infertility treatments involving medical technology. They do this because:
   - they all involve fertilisation taking place apart from the sex act and God intended procreation to come from sex
   - any process using IVF involves some embryos being thrown away when not used, and this is the same as abortion.
2. Other Christians accept IVF and AIH because:
   - the egg and sperm are from the husband and wife
   - technology should be used to give couples the joy of children.

However, they are suspicious of all other techniques, though they have not banned them, because they involve difficulties involving identity of the parents and children wanting information about the donors in later life.

KEY FACTS

Christians have two attitudes to infertility treatments:
1. Some Christians, mainly Roman Catholics, do not allow any of the treatments because they involve either immoral sex or taking the life of unwanted embryos.
2. Other Christians allow IVF and AIH, but are suspicious of all other methods even though they do not ban them.

Remember
- IVF means in-vitro-fertilisation (test tube babies).
- AIH means Artificial Insemination by Husband.
- AID means Artificial Insemination by Donor.

Religion and Medical Issues

5.1.3 The attitudes to infertility treatments of one non-Christian religion

Islam and infertility treatments

MAIN FACTS

Islam accepts IVF and AIH because:
- the egg and sperm are from the husband and wife
- family is necessary for Muslims, and technology can be used to help bring it about
- the unused embryos are not regarded as foetuses until they are fourteen days old.

Islam does not allow any other forms of embryo technology because:
- they deny a child's right to know its natural parents
- they are the same as adoption, which is banned in Islam.

KEY FACTS

Islam allows IVF and AIH because they only involve the husband and wife. Islam does not allow any other forms of infertility treatment because they cause problems concerning the identity of the parents.

Remember
All Muslims should have children because they should follow the example of the Prophet who had children.

Judaism and fertility treatments

MAIN FACTS

IVF and AIH are accepted by all Jews and many would accept egg donation as long as the donor is Jewish. They believe this because:
- having children is very important in Judaism
- the rabbis teach that humans can use the benefits of technology as long as they are within the mitzvot
- the discarded embryos are not regarded as foetuses until they are fourteen days old.

Most Jews would not allow any other form of embryo technology because:
- AID is seen as a form of adultery
- children have a right to know who their natural parents are
- whoever gives birth is the mother, so surrogacy is wrong.

KEY FACTS

All Jews accept IVF and AIH, because having children is very important in Judaism. Some Jews accept all forms of infertility treatments, but some do not accept AID because of problems concerning the identity of the parents.

70 Religion and Medical Issues

5.1.3 The attitudes to infertility treatments of one non-Christian religion

Hinduism and infertility treatments

MAIN FACTS

Hindus allow IVF and AIH because:
- all Hindus are expected to have a family, and technology can be used to bring this about
- the egg and sperm are from the husband and wife
- the discarded embryos had no soul transferred to them.

AID and embryo donation are not allowed because:
- caste is passed down through the father.

Some Hindus would allow egg donation and surrogacy with strict controls.

KEY FACTS

- Some Hindus allow IVF, AIH egg donation and surrogacy because Hindus need to have a family.
- Some Hindus do not allow AID or embryo donation because caste is passed on by the father, but others do allow these.

Sikhism and infertility treatments

MAIN FACTS

Some Sikhs do not allow treatments which involve technology because:
- IVF involves throwing away embryos which Sikhs think is the same as abortion.

Many Sikhs would accept AIH and IVF but not other forms of treatment because:
- it is good to use technology to provide couples with the joy of children as long as the egg and sperm are from the husband and wife
- they think the thrown away embryos are not foetuses as a foetus has to be in the womb to be life.

KEY FACTS

Some Sikhs do not allow any of the treatments because they involve taking the life of unwanted embryos.
Other Sikhs allow IVF and AIH, but are suspicious of all other methods, even though they do not ban them.

5.1.4 Genetic engineering in humans

MAIN FACTS

Genetic diseases affect large numbers of people and are responsible for mental retardation, physical deformities and early deaths. Scientists are using research on gene development and the manipulation of genes to find cures for these diseases. Recently, discoveries in cloning have made it possible to use stem cells to grow healthy genes to replace defective ones. This involves using stem cells from embryos created for IVF, but not used.

In the UK all genetic research into humans is controlled by the Human Fertilisation and Embryology Authority.
Non-religious arguments in favour of genetic engineering include:
- it could cure incurable diseases
- it is an essential part of medical research
- it is being done in most other countries, so rich people would be able to use it anyway.

Non-religious arguments against genetic engineering:
- we do not know what the long-term consequences are likely to be
- if anything went wrong, it could not be reversed
- people might be made to have genetic tests for insurance, jobs etc. to check for genes likely to cause illness.

KEY FACTS

Genetic engineering is finding out which genes cause diseases, such as muscular dystrophy, and then working out how the genes can be changed so that the disease does not develop. Genetic research in the UK is controlled by the Human Fertilisation and Embryology Authority.

Remember
Some genetic researchers outside the UK are offering couples the chance to design their baby – colour of eyes and hair, intelligence etc.

5.1.5 Christian attitudes to genetic engineering

MAIN FACTS

There are three main attitudes to genetic engineering among Christians:

1 Liberal Protestants support genetic engineering as long as it is done to cure disease and not to create perfect humans. They believe this because:
   - Jesus showed that Christians should do all they can to cure disease
   - finding genetic cures is no different from finding drug cures
   - there is a difference between creating cells and creating people
   - embryos cannot be regarded as potential human life until they are fourteen days old
   - they accept the non-religious arguments in favour of genetic engineering.

2 Roman Catholics, and some other Christians, agree with genetic research as long as it does not involve the use of embryos. They believe this because:
   - Jesus showed that Christians should do all they can to cure disease
   - finding genetic cures is no different from finding drug cures
   - life begins at the moment of conception, whether in a womb or a laboratory, and killing life is wrong
   - embryos have been produced by methods with which the Catholic Church disagrees.

3 Some Christians are against all genetic research because:
   - it is trying to 'play God', which is a great sin
   - it is wrong to try to make the Earth perfect, only heaven is perfect
   - they accept all the non-religious arguments against genetic engineering.

KEY FACTS

There are three Christian attitudes to genetic engineering:
1 Some Christians allow all genetic research, as long as it is to find cures for diseases, because Jesus was a healer.
2 Some Christians allow genetic research which does not involve the destruction of embryos, which they believe to be human life.
3 Some Christians ban all genetic research because they believe it is 'playing God'.

Remember
An embryo is a fertilised egg less than fourteen days old, a foetus is an embryo more than fourteen days old.

Religion and Medical Issues 73

5.1.6 The attitudes to genetic engineering of one non-Christian religion

Islam and genetic engineering

MAIN FACTS

Some Muslims are against all genetic engineering because:
- only God has the right to alter people's genetic make-up
- embryo research is the same as abortion, which they do not agree with
- it is playing God which is a great sin
- they accept the non-religious arguments against genetic research.

Some Muslims agree with genetic engineering, as long as it is done to cure diseases and not to create 'perfect' people. They believe this because:
- the Qur'an and hadith teach that Muslims should do all they can to cure disease
- finding genetic cures is no different from finding drug cures
- embryos are not potential life until they are fourteen days old, so research on them is not abortion
- there is a difference between creating cells and creating people
- they also accept the non-religious arguments in favour of genetic engineering.

Is a microscopic embryo in a test tube a human being?

KEY FACTS

There are two Muslim attitudes to genetic engineering:
1. Some Muslims do not allow any form of genetic engineering because they believe it is 'playing God'.
2. Some Muslims allow it, as long as it is to find cures for diseases, because the Qur'an teaches Muslims to cure disease.

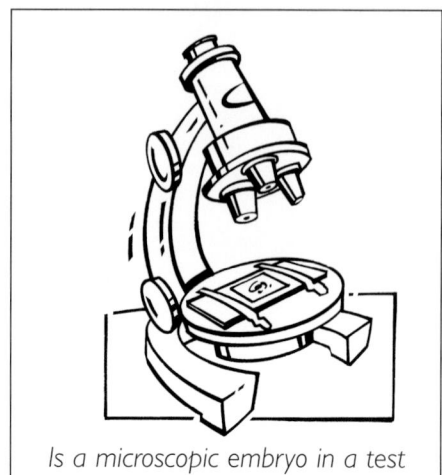

5.1.6 The attitudes to genetic engineering of one non-Christian religion

Judaism and genetic engineering

MAIN FACTS

Orthodox Jews agree with genetic engineering as long as it is done to cure disease and not create 'perfect' people. They believe this because:
- the Talmud and Tenakh teach that Jews should do all they can to cure disease
- finding genetic cures is no different from finding drug cures
- there is a difference between creating cells and creating people.

But they do not allow research using embryos because:
- life begins at the moment of conception, whether in a womb or a laboratory
- killing an embryo is the same as abortion, which they do not agree with
- embryos for research have been created by methods with which Judaism disagrees.

Liberal Jews agree with all forms of genetic research because they believe that embryos are not 'life' until they are fourteen days old.

KEY FACTS

- Orthodox Jews allow genetic research, as long as it does not involve the use of embryos, because Jews should cure disease but not take life.
- Liberal Jews allow all forms of genetic research, as long as it is to find a cure for disease, because Jews should cure disease, and embryos are not considered life until they are fourteen days old.

5.1.6 The attitudes to genetic engineering of one non-Christian religion

Hinduism and genetic engineering

MAIN FACTS

Most Hindus agree with genetic engineering as long as it is done to cure disease and not to create 'perfect humans'. They believe this because:
- Hindus should do all they can to cure disease
- discovering cures is part of the dharma of doctors
- there is a difference between creating cells and creating people
- embryos cannot be regarded as 'life' until they are fourteen days old.

Some Hindus are opposed to all forms of genetic engineering because:
- it is breaking the law of karma. The genetic structure of people is what the law of karma says they should have on the basis of their previous lives
- genetic engineering could be doing violence to a person's genetic make-up and so would be banned by ahimsa.

KEY FACTS

- Most Hindus agree with all genetic research in order to cure disease, because Hindus should try to cure diseases.
- Some Hindus are against all genetic engineering as they think it is trying to change the law of karma.

Sikhism and genetic engineering

MAIN FACTS

Most Sikhs agree with genetic engineering to cure disease, but not to create 'perfect humans' because:
- there is a difference between creating cells and creating people
- Sikhs should do all they can to cure disease.

Some Sikhs are against genetic engineering because:
- changing a person's genes could change their chances of gaining mukti
- they believe embryos are people.

KEY FACTS

Most Sikhs agree with genetic research because Sikhs should try to cure diseases. Some Sikhs are against all genetic engineering because it is changing people's karma.

> **!**
> **Remember**
> Samsara is the process of reincarnation, by becoming God-centred Sikhs hope to end the process by gaining mukti.

5.1.7 Transplant surgery

MAIN FACTS

This is using organs from one person to replace defective organs in another. They may be taken from a living person (e.g. a kidney transplant) or a dead person (e.g. a heart transplant). Advances in medicine have made transplant surgery very effective.

Non-religious arguments in favour of transplants
- It is an effective method of curing life-threatening or disabling diseases.
- It uses organs that would otherwise disappear.
- It allows people to help others after their death.
- It brings life out of death.

Non-religious arguments against transplants
- It is very expensive and uses a lot of medical skill and money for very few people.
- It raises moral problems concerning the actual time of someone's death and whether surgeons try to keep alive someone whose organs can be used.
- It encourages the sale of organs from LEDCs to the West.
- It diverts resources from the prevention of diseases and less expensive cures.

KEY FACTS

Transplant surgery is using healthy organs from a donor to replace a dying organ in a patient. Some people agree with it because it can give life to someone from someone who has died. Other people disagree with it because it causes concerns about when a donor is pronounced dead.

5.1.8 Christian attitudes to transplant surgery

MAIN FACTS

Most Christians agree with transplant surgery, but would disagree with organs being bought from poor people.
They believe this because:
- those who believe in immortality of the soul believe that the body is not needed after death
- those who believe in resurrection believe that God will not need the organs to raise the body
- leaving organs for others is a way of loving your neighbour
- the Bible says the poor should not be exploited.

Some Christians agree with transplants using organs from living people, but not from dead people. They would also not allow payment for organs. They believe this because:
- transplanting organs from the dead to the living is 'playing God', which is a great sin
- donating your living organs is a way of loving your neighbour
- paying for organs is exploiting the poor, which is banned in the Bible.

Some Christians do not agree with transplants at all and do not carry donor cards because:
- they believe it ignores the sanctity of life
- they believe it is 'playing God', which is a great sin
- they agree with all the non-religious arguments against transplants.

KEY FACTS

There are three attitudes among Christians:
1. Some Christians agree with both types of transplant surgery, because they believe the body is not needed after death, but they do not agree with buying organs from poor people.
2. Some Christians only agree with living transplants because using dead people is 'playing God'.
3. Some Christians believe that all forms of transplant surgery are wrong because they are 'playing God'.

Remember
Organs such as a single kidney can be taken from a live donor, organs such as hearts and livers can only come from dead donors.

5.1.9 The attitudes to transplant surgery of one non-Christian religion

Islam and transplant surgery

MAIN FACTS

Most Muslims do not agree with transplant surgery because:
- the Shari'ah teaches that nothing should be removed from the body after death
- it is 'playing God', which is a great sin
- the Qur'an teaches that only God has the right to give and take life
- they would agree with all the non-religious arguments against transplants.

Some Muslims allow transplants using organs from a living donor who is a close relative because:
- some Muslim lawyers have said it is allowed
- the Muslim Law Council of the United Kingdom says that Muslims can carry donor cards and have transplants
- Islam aims to do good and help people.

KEY FACTS

- Most Muslims do not agree with any transplant surgery because they believe they need all their organs for the Last Day.
- Some Muslims allow transplants from close relatives because this is allowed by Muslim lawyers.

5.1.9 The attitudes to transplant surgery of one non-Christian religion

Judaism and transplant surgery

MAIN FACTS

Most Jews agree with transplants using living donors, but do not agree with using organs from dead people, or organs being paid for. They believe this because:
- organs such as the heart are an essential part of the individual God has created
- organs from living donors are not as vital and can be used to obey the mitzvah to preserve life
- paying for organs is exploiting the poor, which is banned by the Tenakh
- it is playing God which is a great sin.

Some Jews are against all forms of transplant surgery. They believe this because:
- transplanting organs is breaking the mitzvot on the sanctity of life
- having non-Jewish organs could change a Jew into a non-Jew
- they agree with all the non-religious arguments against transplants.

KEY FACTS

- Most Jews agree with transplants from living donors, but not from the dead or non-Jews because organs from non-Jews would alter a person's Jewishness.
- Some Jews are against all transplants because they think they are breaking the laws on the sanctity of life.

Remember

Sanctity of life means that life is holy and belongs to God alone.

5.1.9 The attitudes to transplant surgery of one non-Christian religion

Hinduism and transplant surgery

MAIN FACTS

Most Hindus agree with transplant surgery and would carry donor cards. They have this attitude because:
- the soul leaves the body on death, so what happens to the organs does not matter
- the soul is the immortal part of any individual, so any organs added to the body do not matter
- they agree with all the non-religious arguments in favour of transplants.

Some Hindus are against any form of transplant surgery because:
- transplants break the law of karma – diseased organs are part of a person's karma
- taking an organ from someone is making a violent act towards that person, which is against the teaching of ahimsa
- poor people will be tempted to sell their organs to provide money for the family.

KEY FACTS

- Most Hindus allow transplant surgery because they believe that the soul leaves the body at death, so the organs are not needed.
- Some Hindus do not allow transplant surgery because they think it is breaking the law of karma.

! Remember

Rich people who are ill can offer very poor Indians a fortune for their family to donate organs such as a heart!

5.1.9 The attitudes to transplant surgery of one non-Christian religion

Sikhism and transplant surgery

MAIN FACTS

Most Sikhs agree with transplants using dead or living donors, but do not agree with organs being paid for. They believe this because:
- organ donation is a form of sewa (service) which is very important for Sikhs
- Guru Nanak said people should leave something to make their good deeds carry on after death
- Sikhs believe the physical body is not needed after death.

A few Sikhs do not agree with transplant surgery in any form. They have this attitude because:
- it raises the problem of when someone is dead (in heart transplants the heart is removed before it has stopped beating)
- it raises the problem of whether surgeons who have a patient desperate for a transplant will do their best to save the life of a potential donor
- it tempts poor people to sell their organs to rich people.

KEY FACTS

Most Sikhs agree with both forms of transplant surgery because the body is not needed after death and donation is a form of sewa.

A few Sikhs do not agree with any transplant surgery because of concerns about when someone is dead and pressures on the living to donate their organs.

PRACTICE QUESTIONS ✓

a Outline the medical treatments available for infertility. *(4 marks)*

b Explain why there are different attitudes among Christians to transplant surgery. *(8 marks)*

c 'Only God should interfere with our genes.'
Do you agree? Give reasons for your opinion, showing you have considered another point of view. In your answer, you should refer to at least one religion. *(8 marks)*

Religion and Science

SECTION 5.2

5.2.1 Biblical cosmology

KEY WORD

Cosmology the study of the origin and structure of the universe.

! Remember

The seventh day is the day of rest because God created the universe in six days.

MAIN FACTS

There are two accounts of the creation in Genesis:
1. Chapter one says God created the universe in six days in the following order: heaven and Earth, dry land, plants and trees, sun, moon and stars, fish and birds, animals and finally humans
2. Chapter two says God created the universe in the following order: heaven and Earth, man, trees and vegetation, birds and animals, Eve from Adam's rib.

KEY FACTS

The biblical cosmology is in Genesis. Chapter one says that God created everything in six days and rested on the seventh. Chapter two is slightly different and is about Adam and Eve.

5.2.2 Different Christian attitudes to the biblical cosmology

MAIN FACTS

There are three Christian attitudes to the biblical cosmology.

1. Some Christians (literalists, or fundamentalists) believe that the Bible is the words of God which he dictated. This means that every word in the Bible is true and so Genesis 1 and 2 are facts. They think Genesis 1 outlines all creation, and Genesis 2 is just about Day 6 of creation.
2. Some Christians (conservatives) believe that the Bible is the Word of God, but not his actual words. They think the writers were guided by God, but they used their own words. Conservatives think Genesis 1 and 2 give an outline of creation, not total scientific fact. They think Genesis 1 is fairly factual, but Genesis 2 and 3 are stories explaining how suffering and evil came to the world.
3. Some Christians (liberals) believe that the Bible is words about God, the Bible writers were people who had special experiences of God. They think the Bible cosmology is a story whose message is that the universe was created by God, and is good. They think Genesis 2 is a different story of creation by a different person about some other truths. Liberal Christians accept the Big Bang and evolution.

KEY FACTS

There are different attitudes to the cosmology because of different attitudes to the Bible.
- Some Christians believe the Bible is the words of God so they accept the cosmology as fact.
- Some Christians believe the Bible is inspired by God and so they see the cosmology as faith based on fact.
- Some Christians believe the Bible is human ideas about God and so they see the cosmology as a story.

5.2.3 The cosmology of one non-Christian religion

The Islamic cosmology

> **MAIN FACTS**
>
> There are two Muslim views on the origins of the universe and humans:
>
> #### 1. The traditional view
> Some Muslims believe that:
> - God created the universe and everything in it in six days
> - God created Adam and his wife as the first humans
> - all humans are descended from Adam and Eve.
>
> #### 2. The modern view
> Some Muslims believe that God created the universe in a more gradual way which fits in with evolution because:
> - the Arabic words in the Qur'an mean six ages not six days
> - there is no order of creation in the Qur'an
> - the Qur'an clearly shows that in these six ages, God created the universe, then life on Earth and finally humans.
>
> **KEY FACTS**
>
> There are two Islamic cosmologies:
> - In one version God created the universe in six days and all humans are descended from Adam and Eve.
> - In the other version God created the universe in six ages and Adam was the first human created by God.

! Remember

Most Muslims believe that God continues to create human life by inserting the soul into the embryo in the womb.

5.2.3 The cosmology of one non-Christian religion

The Jewish cosmology

MAIN FACTS

There are two accounts of the creation in Genesis:
1. Chapter one says God created the universe in six days in the following order: heaven and Earth, dry land, plants and trees, sun, moon and stars, fish and birds, animals and finally humans.
2. Chapter two says God created the universe in the following order: heaven and Earth, man, trees and vegetation, birds and animals, Eve from Adam's rib.

Orthodox Jews believe that the second account is just explaining the first and that both are the word of God.

Liberal Jews believe that the two accounts are both stories to explain how God created the world and are not meant to be taken literally.

KEY FACTS

The Jewish cosmology is in Genesis. Chapter one says that God created everything in six days and rested on the seventh. Chapter two is slightly different and is about Adam and Eve. Orthodox Jews believe that chapter two explains chapter one and both are factual. Many Liberal Jews believe both are stories explaining how God created the world.

Remember
Orthodox Jews accept and follow all the mitzvot. Liberal Jews believe the mitzvot should be adapted to modern life.

The Hindu cosmology

MAIN FACTS

There are two different accounts of how the universe and humans began:
1. One account is based on stories in the Vedas. It says that the whole universe came from Purusha who sacrificed himself to create the universe. The story is the basis of the caste system as well, since the higher castes came from the higher parts of his body.
2. The other account is based on philosophical ideas in the Upanishads. It claims that Brahman is the force behind the universe and the creation of the universe is like Samsara. The universe comes into being, it lives, it dies, then it is reborn and so on in an unending process.

Remember
Samsara is the Hindu cycle of life and re-birth – every end is a new beginning.

86 Religion and Science

5.2.3 The cosmology of one non-Christian religion

> ### KEY FACTS
>
> There are two Hindu cosmologies:
> 1. The Vedas story says the universe came from the body of Purusha.
> 2. The Upanishad cosmology says the universe is Brahman, and it is born and dies in cycles, like Samsara.

The Sikh cosmology

> ### MAIN FACTS
>
> Sikhs believe that God existed before He created the universe. There was darkness and chaos for millions of years. There were mists and clouds. Nothing existed except God. Then God willed the creation of the universe. He became manifest: Sargun. He spread out Himself in nature.
>
> Sikhs believe that the actual time and process of creation can never be known. Sikh thinkers have claimed that creation could have been sudden evolution. However it happened, Sikhs believe that the universe is not an illusion. It is reality because of the presence of God in it.
>
> God created life and humans with the cycle of samsara as the path to mukti.
>
> ### KEY FACTS
>
> Sikhs believe that God existed in a state of contemplation before the creation of the universe. The universe was created by God in a mysterious way. He is within the universe and created humans and the cycle of existence as a way to mukti.

Remember
Mukti is the Sikh belief in liberation from the cycle of reincarnation to live with God.

Religion and Science 87

5.2.4 The scientific cosmology

MAIN FACTS

Science says that matter is eternal and has always existed. About 15 billion years ago the matter of the universe exploded with a Big Bang. After this, scientific forces such as gravity compressed the exploded matter into stars and solar systems. As part of this process our solar system was formed about five billion years ago. Chemical reactions on the Earth led to life forms beginning, and the process of evolution over 2.5 billion years led to the arrival of humans about 2.5 million years ago. The scientific cosmology does not need God to explain the universe or the existence of humans.

KEY FACTS

Science says that matter is eternal and that the universe began when this matter exploded. The solar system came out of the explosion and the nature of the Earth allowed life to develop through evolution.

Remember
Big Bang is the theory about the origin of the universe according to science.

5.2.5 Christian attitudes to the scientific cosmology

MAIN FACTS

Some Christians (creationists) reject the scientific cosmology. They say it is wrong and Genesis is correct. They claim that evidence for the Big Bang, evolution etc. is better explained by creationism and Noah's flood.

Some Christians (conservatives) claim that both the Bible and science are correct and that one of God's days could be millions or billions of years.

Some Christians (liberals) believe that the scientific cosmology is the true one and the Bible is just a story. They believe that the scientific cosmology needs God to make it work. They believe that God set off the Big Bang at just the right micro-second for the universe and humans to develop.

KEY FACTS

Christians have three attitudes to the scientific cosmology:
- Some Christians say it is wrong and the biblical cosmology is fact because it is the word of God.
- Some Christians think that both science and the Bible are true because one of God's days could be billions of years.
- Some Christians believe the scientific cosmology needs God to explain how the Earth and humans came into being.

Remember
Creationist Christians believe Adam would have looked about 20 when he was one second old and trees would have had rings showing them to be hundreds of years old when they were one second old.

5.2.6 The attitudes of one non-Christian religion to the scientific cosmology

Muslim responses to the scientific cosmology

MAIN FACTS

Muslims who believe in the six day creation believe that the Qur'an is correct and that science is wrong.

Muslims who believe in the six age creation believe that the scientific cosmology and the Qur'an are the same. God created the matter of the universe and the laws of science, which led to the creation of the universe and life. They believe that God intervened to breathe his life into humans.

KEY FACTS

- Muslims who believe in the six day creation think science is wrong.
- Muslims who believe in the six age creation think the scientific cosmology is just a different form of the true Islamic cosmology.

Jewish responses to the scientific cosmology

MAIN FACTS

A few Orthodox Jews reject the scientific cosmology. They say that it is wrong and that Genesis is correct. They claim that the evidence for the Big Bang, evolution etc. is better explained by creationism and Noah's flood.

Most Orthodox Jews and some Liberal Jews claim that both the Bible and science are correct and that one of God's days could be millions or billions of years.

Most Liberal Jews believe that the scientific cosmology is the true one and the Bible is just a story. They believe that the scientific cosmology needs God to make it work. They believe that God set off the Big Bang at just the right microsecond for the universe and humans to develop.

KEY FACTS

There are three Jewish attitudes:
1. Some Jews say the scientific cosmology is wrong and the biblical cosmology is fact because it is the word of God.
2. Some Jews think that both science and the Bible are true because one of God's days could be billions of years.
3. Some Jews believe the scientific cosmology is fact, but needs God to explain how the Earth and humans came into being.

5.2.6 The attitudes of one non-Christian religion to the scientific cosmology

Hindu responses to the scientific cosmology

> **MAIN FACTS**
>
> Some Hindus never think about the scientific cosmology. They believe the Purusha story is the way creation happened. Many Hindus believe that the scientific cosmology is just the same as those in the Upanishads. The Big Bang is the way Brahman began the current universe. The universe will eventually contract and then explode again to form a new universe and so on forever.
>
> **KEY FACTS**
>
> - Some Hindus believe the Vedic story of Purusha and do not think about science.
> - Many Hindus believe the scientific cosmology is just a form of the Upanishad cosmology.

Sikh responses to the scientific cosmology

> **MAIN FACTS**
>
> Most Sikhs accept the scientific cosmology as the way in which God created his universe because:
> - the scriptures are mysterious about how God created the universe
> - the scientific cosmology is so remarkable that the Big Bang and evolution could only have happened if God made them happen.
>
> **KEY FACTS**
>
> Most Sikhs believe the scientific cosmology is fact. They feel it explains the mystery of God's creation because it needs God to explain how the Earth and humans came into being.

5.2.7 Connections between science and religion

MAIN FACTS

There are many differences between science and religion:
- science deals with the material; religion deals with the spiritual
- science is based on facts; religion is based on beliefs
- science is based on recent discoveries; religion is based on holy books written thousands of years ago.

However, there are also many similarities:

Science:
- is based on everything having an explanation
- says there are invisible forces which affect the way things behave, e.g. gravity, magnetism
- is based on belief – a scientist believes that nothing happens by chance and everything can be explained by scientific methods
- says theories should be tested by experiment.

Religion:
- believes everything has an explanation and the explanation is God
- believes that God is an invisible force which affects everything
- is based on belief – nothing happens by chance, everything can be explained by God
- says (according to religious experts) religions should be tested by the effects they have on people's lives.

KEY FACTS

Science and religion have some differences, as science deals with matter and religion deals with the unseen spiritual side, but they also have similarities:
- Both believe everything has an explanation.
- Both believe life is affected by unseen forces.
- Both believe in testing theories.

Remember
No one can see the force of magnetism, only its effects. Religious people say it's the same with God.

5.2.8 How some scientists see science as leading to, or supporting, belief in God

MAIN FACTS

1 Many scientists are led to believe in God by the scientific cosmology because:
   - the Big Bang had to be at exactly the right micro-second
   - the way stars are formed and spread carbon and oxygen around the universe needs a creator to organise
   - the way life requires carbon to be able to bond with four other atoms and water molecules could not have happened by chance.

Therefore the Big Bang and evolution could only have happened if God made them happen.

2 Many religious scientists think DNA is too complicated and beautiful to be an accident. They also see the hand of God in the laws of science without which there would be chaos.

3 Many mathematicians think that the whole universe works on mathematical principles which they discover through research. If the principles are there waiting to be discovered, they must have been put there by God.

4 Other religious scientists say that science is based on everything having an explanation, but if this is true, the universe itself must have an explanation and that could only be God.

KEY FACTS

Some scientists find studying science leads them to believe in God because the way the Big Bang and evolution led to humans, the laws of science, the mathematical principles on which the universe is based, and the way everything has an explanation seem to require a being like God.

PRACTICE QUESTIONS ✓

a Describe the biblical cosmology in Genesis. *(4 marks)*
b Explain why there are different attitudes to this cosmology among Christians. *(8 marks)*
c 'Science has disproved religion.'
  Do you agree? Give reasons for your opinion, showing you have considered another point of view. In your answer, you should refer to at least one religion. *(8 marks)*

FULL MARK ANSWERS TO PRACTICE QUESTIONS

RELIGION AND SOCIAL RESPONSIBILITY

a State ONE of the Ten Commandments. *(2 marks)*
Do not kill.

This would gain full marks because it is a correct commandment.

b Give an outline of the Christian attitude that religion and politics should be kept separate. *(6 marks)*
When Jesus was asked about paying taxes to the Romans, he said that Christians should give Caesar what is Caesar's and God what is God's. Many Christians think this means that politics should be separate from religion and that religion is about looking after your soul and your life after death, while politics is about this life.

This would gain full marks because it is an organised outline of the Christian attitude – showing Jesus' teaching and how it leads to the separation of religion and politics.

c Explain why the Bible is important to Christians in making moral decisions. *(8 marks)*
Many Christians believe that the Bible is the word of God. This means that the Bible is giving them God's commandments. They are therefore bound to use it as guidance on how to behave. The New Testament is the second part of the Bible and it contains the teachings and guidance given by Jesus on how to live the Christian life. Christians believe that Jesus is God's son and therefore they must follow his guidance on how to live. The Bible also contains such moral guidance as the Ten Commandments and the Sermon on the Mount. For all these reasons, the Bible is important for Christians when they make their moral decisions.

This would gain full marks because it is a comprehensive and coherent explanation which develops three reasons for the Bible's importance.

d 'Your conscience is the best guide for deciding what is right and what is wrong.'
Do you agree? Give reasons for your opinion, showing you have considered another point of view. In your answer, you should refer to Christianity. *(4 marks)*

I can see why some people would agree with this statement because it is your conscience that makes you feel guilty when you have done bad things. Also, many Christians believe that conscience is God speaking to you and listening to God must be the best way of making moral decisions.

However, I do not agree with this statement because it seems to me that you can justify anything by saying that your conscience told you to do it. I think the Bible and the teachings of the Church are a better guide to deciding what is right and what is wrong because everyone knows what they say. If people use their conscience, then everyone could have different ideas about what is right and what is wrong and that would lead to chaos. We need to know that everyone thinks it is wrong to murder, or we would not feel safe to go out. So I disagree with the statement.

This would gain full marks because it gives an alternative point of view, then it says what is wrong with that point of view in order to come to a personal opinion.

RELIGION AND THE ENVIRONMENT

a What does the word conservation mean? *(2 marks)*

Preserve or keep safe.

This would gain full marks because it is a correct definition.

b Choose ONE religion other than Christianity and outline its teachings on creation. *(6 marks)*

Islam teaches that God created the universe, the Earth and people out of nothing. He created everything as a unity. God created Adam as the first human who was different from the angels because he was given free will. Adam misused his free will and sinned and was thrown out of the garden. He repented of his sin at Arafat and was made the first prophet of God.

This would gain full marks because it is an organised outline of Muslim teaching making more than three points.

c Explain why some Christians are opposed to medical research being carried out on animals. *(8 marks)*

Some Christians are against using animals in medical research because the Bible teaches that animals are a part of God's creation, and according to Genesis, God created animals before he created humans. This means that animals are at least as important as humans to God. Also in the Gospels, there is the teaching of Jesus on non-violence. Jesus said that even the death of a sparrow does not go unnoticed by God. If God notices the death of a sparrow in the street, how much more will he notice the deaths of animals in research? These are all reasons why Christians should not harm animals and if they should not harm animals, then they should not do medical research on animals.

This would gain full marks because it outlines two teachings and gives developed explanations of why they make some Christians opposed to medical research on animals.

d 'If religious people really cared about the environment, they would stop using cars and washing machines.'
Do you agree? Give reasons for your opinion, showing you have considered another point of view. In your answer, you should refer to at least one religion. *(4 marks)*

I can see why some Christians may agree with this statement because they believe they are in charge of God's creation and it is their duty to pass on the environment in a better condition than they found it. They may think that cars and washing machines pollute the environment and should not be used.

However, I disagree with the statement because of the effects if all religious people stopped using such things. All the people involved in the manufacture of cars and washing machines would be put out of work and become poor. Transport would be totally altered and, for example, vicars would not be able to get to funerals. I am sure religious people have to look at the consequences of their actions. In Genesis it says that God made the Earth for humans and so I disagree with the statement.

This would gain full marks because it gives an alternative point of view, then it says what is wrong with that point of view in order to come to a personal opinion.

RELIGION: PEACE AND CONFLICT

This would gain full marks because it is a correct definition.

a What does the word pacifism mean? *(2 marks)*
Refusing to fight in wars.

b Outline different attitudes to war in Christianity. *(6 marks)*
Some Christians believe that they should work for peace by refusing to fight in wars. They believe Christians should be pacifists because Jesus taught Christians to love their enemies. Some Christians believe that the way to bring peace is to be prepared to fight in 'just wars'. They will fight to defend the weak and to bring peace to the world because this has always been the Church's teaching.

This would gain full marks because it is an organised outline identifying just war and making three points about just wars.

c Choose ONE area of conflict in the world and explain why the conflict is happening. *(8 marks)*
The conflict between Israel and Palestine could perhaps go back thousands of years. Israel claims that the Jewish people were illegally expelled from their homeland by the Romans in 132CE and that as they had lived there for 1500 years before that, the land is theirs. The Palestinians claim they have been in the land since it was captured by the Arabs in 636CE and so the land is theirs. However, the real cause of the conflict lies in the ending of the First World War when the British Government promised the Jews a national homeland and also promised the Palestinians a national state. In the 1920s and 1930s, Jews settled in Palestine and in 1948 made their own state of Israel, forcing the Palestinians into special areas or into the Palestinian state of Jordan. The Palestinians have never accepted the right of Israel to be a state and have been fighting for their own state ever since.

This would gain full marks because it is a comprehensive and coherent explanation which outlines more than four reasons for the conflict.

d 'Religious people should never argue with their families.'
Do you agree? Give reasons for your opinion, showing you have considered another point of view. In your answer, you should refer to at least one religion. *(4 marks)*

I can see why some Muslims and Christians would agree with this statement because of the teaching of their religion on the family, which says that children should obey their parents and so there should be no arguments in a family.

However, I disagree with the statement because it takes too simple a view of family life. For example, Christianity and Islam both teach that religion should come before the family. If a Christian wants to become a priest and his family want him to marry, then there will be argument with the family, and the Church would say that the man is right to argue with his family because the call to be a priest must come before the family. In the same way, in Islam there could be family argument if a father was running a shop which sold alcohol. So I disagree with the statement, even though I think religious people should try not to argue with their families.

This would gain full marks because it gives an alternative point of view, then it says what is wrong with that point of view in order to come to a personal opinion.

Full mark answers to practice questions

RELIGION: CRIME AND PUNISHMENT

This would gain full marks because it names two correct theories.

a Name TWO theories of punishment. *(2 marks)*
Retribution and deterrence.

b Outline Christian teaching on forgiveness. *(6 marks)*

This would gain full marks because it is an organised outline which states three teachings.

Christian teaching is that God offers forgiveness to anyone who repents of their sins. In the Roman Catholic tradition, God's forgiveness comes via the priest through acts of contrition and penance. Christians are expected to forgive people who wrong them. They promise this in the Lord's Prayer and St Peter was told by Jesus to forgive his brother up to seventy-seven times.

c Choose ONE religion other than Christianity and explain why there are different attitudes to capital punishment among its followers. *(8 marks)*

This would gain full marks because it is a comprehensive and coherent explanation which explains the contrast between the Qur'anic references to capital punishment and blood money. It then explains why liberal Muslims have a different attitude.

Islam permits capital punishment because it is the punishment stated for certain crimes in the Qur'an. So in the Shari'ah (Muslim holy law) certain crimes have to be punished by capital punishment. However, the Muslim theory of justice also involves the victims of crime and thinks they have rights in the punishment of their attackers. So it is possible for the relatives of a murdered person to substitute a money payment for the death penalty.

This is one reason why there are different attitudes to capital punishment. Another is that more liberal Muslims think that capital punishment is out of date and that it is not necessary to follow the teaching of the Qur'an on punishment because it was intended for long ago.

d 'Committing a sin is as bad as committing a crime.'
Do you agree? Give reasons for your opinion, showing you have considered another point of view. In your answer, you should refer to at least one religion. *(4 marks)*

This would gain full marks because it gives an alternative point of view, then it says what is wrong with that point of view in order to come to a personal opinion.

Some religious people would agree with this statement because they believe that sins and crimes are the same thing, and as both are against God's will, they are both evil and are as bad as each other.

However, I do not agree because I think there is a difference between a sin and a crime. A crime is something that is against the law, whereas a sin is something against God's will. This means that, for example, Catholics would regard remarriage after divorce as a sin and I cannot see how that is as bad as committing a crime such as stealing from an old lady. If a marriage has broken up, how can it be evil to fall in love again? I think that crimes are worse than sins because they have an effect on the whole of society, whereas sins only affect the individual's relationship with God.

96 Full mark answers to practice questions

RELIGION AND MEDICAL ISSUES

a Outline the medical treatments available for infertility. *(4 marks)*

There is a wide range of treatments available for infertility. In-vitro-fertilisation is when the man's sperm and woman's egg are fertilised in a laboratory and then replaced in the womb. Artificial insemination by husband is when the husband's sperm is put into the wife's womb by a doctor. This leads to fertilisation.

Artificial insemination by donor is when sperm from an unknown man is put into the woman's womb. This leads to fertilisation. Egg donation is when an unknown person's egg is fertilised by the man's sperm and then put into the woman's womb. Embryo donation is when egg and sperm from unknown donors are fertilised and then put into the woman's womb.

This would gain full marks because it is an organised outline which correctly defines more than four treatments.

b Explain why there are different attitudes among Christians to transplant surgery. *(8 marks)*

Most Christians agree with transplant surgery, but would disagree with organs being bought from poor people. They believe this because those who believe in immortality of the soul believe that the body is not needed after death. Similarly, those who believe in resurrection believe that God will not need the organs to raise the body. They also believe that leaving organs for others is a way of loving your neighbour.

Some Christians agree with transplants using organs from living people, but not from dead people. They would also not allow payment for organs. They believe this because transplanting organs from the dead to the living is 'playing God', which is a great sin. However, donating your living organs is a way of loving your neighbour. They think that paying for organs is exploiting the poor, which is banned in the Bible.

This would gain full marks because two different attitudes are given with at least two reasons for each attitude.

c 'Only God should interfere with our genes.'

Do you agree? Give reasons for your opinion, showing you have considered another point of view. In your answer, you should refer to at least one religion. *(8 marks)*

Some Christians would agree with this statement because they think that genetic research is trying to 'play God', which is a great sin. They believe that it is wrong to try to make the Earth perfect, only heaven is perfect.

Some Muslims would also agree because they believe only God has the right to alter people's genetic make-up. Also, embryo research involves abortion. Some Hindus are opposed to all forms of genetic research because it is breaking the law of karma. The genetic structure of people is what the law of karma says they should have on the basis of their previous lives.

However, I disagree with such views. Jesus showed that Christians should do all they can to cure disease and that finding genetic cures is no different from finding drug cures. After all, there is a big difference between creating cells and creating people. I, and many other Christians, believe that embryos are not foetuses until they are fourteen days old. Anyone who has seen people suffering from muscular dystrophy, Parkinson's, Alzheimer's or any other terrible disease that may be cured by genetic research could not read such religious teachings as the Parable of the Sheep and Goats and be opposed to genetic research.

I believe that God gave us our brains to make the world a better place. If genetic engineering to cure diseases is wrong, surely research on animals to provide cures for cancer is wrong, but I don't see many religious people refusing chemotherapy if they have cancer!

This would gain full marks because it gives an alternative point of view, then it says what is wrong with that point of view in order to come to a personal opinion. It uses religious reasons.

Full mark answers to practice questions

The Quality of Written Communication

This would gain full marks because:
- it gained more than 14 marks showing that it presents relevant information in a form that suits its purpose
- the spelling, punctuation and grammar are what would be expected of a grade C GCSE candidate
- it is written in a formal English style using sentences and paragraphs.

RELIGION AND SCIENCE

a Describe the biblical cosmology in Genesis. *(4 marks)*

There are two different cosmologies in Genesis. In chapter one God created the universe and everything in it in six days. He created heaven and Earth, light and day on day one, then he separated the Earth from the sky on day two, dry land, plants and trees on day three, the sun, moon and stars on day four, fish and birds on day five and then animals and humans on day six.

In Genesis chapter two, God created heaven and Earth, then Adam, then trees and vegetation, then birds and animals and finally Eve because Adam was lonely.

This would gain full marks because it is an organised description of the two accounts in Genesis.

b Explain why there are different attitudes to this cosmology among Christians. *(8 marks)*

Some Christians believe the Biblical cosmology and claim that the Big Bang and evolution are wrong because the Bible is the word of God. They also claim that creationism (the idea that at the moment of creation the Grand Canyon would have looked 2 billion years old, but would only have been one second old), is a better explanation of the scientific evidence than evolution.

Some Christians believe that the biblical cosmology could have given a day as meaning millions or even billions of years and they try to believe in both the Bible and science.

Other Christians believe that the biblical cosmology is just a story. They believe that the Bible was written by humans about God and so is not always factually accurate. They see the story of the cosmology as important because it shows that God created everything. However, they think the scientific cosmology is more correct. However, they believe that science needs God to make it work, God had to set off the Big Bang at just the right microsecond for the universe and human beings to develop.

So science and attitudes to the nature of the Bible are why Christians have different attitudes to the biblical cosmology.

This would gain full marks because it is a comprehensive and coherent explanation of the three different Christian attitudes.

c 'Science has disproved religion.'

Do you agree? Give reasons for your opinion, showing you have considered another point of view. In your answer, you should refer to at least one religion. *(8 marks)*

Some Christians might disagree with this because they feel that the Bible is the word of God and proves that religion is correct. Similarly, some Muslims would argue that the Qur'an is the only evidence needed to show that religion is true. There are also many religious believers who are scientists and who claim that science shows the existence of God. They would point to the complexity of life originating from the Big Bang and evolution to argue that there must be a God in control of science.

However, I would disagree with them because I feel that there is a considerable amount of evidence about science disproving religion. Astronauts have been into space and they have not seen God anywhere, therefore where is God? If God is nowhere, then religion has been disproved. When books such as the Bible and the Qur'an have scientific methods applied to them it can be seen that they have contradictions, which they could not have if they had been written by God. As far as Big Bang and evolution are concerned, it seems to me that religious scientists deliberately avoid the chances and cruelties involved in the Big Bang. Would God have wasted his time in allowing dinosaurs to develop and be killed off with such cruelty?

On the evidence, I believe that science has indeed disproved religion.

This would gain full marks because it gives an alternative point of view, then it says what is wrong with that point of view in order to come to a personal opinion. It uses religious reasons.

The Quality of Written Communication

This would gain full marks because:
- it gained more than 14 marks showing that it presents relevant information in a form that suits its purpose
- the spelling, punctuation and grammar are what would be expected of a grade C GCSE candidate
- it is written in a formal English style using sentences and paragraphs.